Cootie Shots

is about people not being afraid
of what they don't understand.

Christian Watkins
November 16, 1999

CoOOTIe SHOTs

THEATRICAL INOCULATIONS AGAINST BIGOTRY FOR KIDS, PARENTS AND TEACHERS PLAYS, POEMS & SONGS

NORMA BOWLES, Editor & **MARK E. ROSENTHAL**, Associate Editor

A Fringe Benefits book
Theatre Communications Group, New York

Cootie Shots: Theatrical Inoculations Against Bigotry for Kids, Parents and Teachers is published by Theatre Communications Group Inc., 355 Lexington Avenue, New York, NY 10017-6603.

The publisher wishes to thank the following:

(p 8–11) *The Duke Who Outlawed Jelly Beans*, adapted from Johnny Valentine with illustrations by Lynette Schmidt, copyright © 1991. Reprinted by permission of Alyson Wonderland on behalf of Johnny Valentine and Lynette Schmidt. (p 18–19) *That's a Family!* directed by Debra Chasnoff, Executive Producer, Helen S. Cohen, Women's Educational Media. (p 32) Illustration copyright © 1997 by James C. Ransome from *I Have a Dream* by Dr. Martin Luther King, Jr. Reprinted by permission of Scholastic, Inc. (p 39) *The Golden Rule* by Norman Rockwell by permission of the Norman Rockwell Family Trust. (p 66, 69) Illustrations from *Wings* by Christopher Myers, copyright © 2000 by Christopher Myers. Reprinted by permission of Scholastic, Inc. (p 79) *Opposition* from *Yes Yes No No* by Tony Kushner, copyright © 1985 and 1987 by the author. (p 89) Andy Warhol, "High Heels" copyright © 2000 by the Andy Warhol Foundation for the Visual Arts/ ARS, New York. (p 122) Anthony photo copyright © CORBIS. (p 123) Chavez photo copyright © Bettmann / CORBIS. (p 124) Parks photo copyright © Bettmann / CORBIS. (p 125) Milk photo copyright © Roger Ressmeyer / CORBIS. (p 126–127) Illustration by Ned Bittinger from *The Blue and the Gray* by Eve Bunting. Illustration © 1996 by Ned Bittinger. Reprinted by permission of Scholastic, Inc. (p 130) Tipton photo by Kitty Oakes. Used by permission of the Stanford University Library. (p 132) We'wha photo courtesy of National Anthropological Archives, Smithsonian Institution. (p 139) Art copyright © The Estate of Keith Haring.

This publication is made possible in part with public funds from the New York State Council on the Arts, a State Agency.

TCG Books are exclusively distributed to the book trade by Consortium Book Sales and Distribution, 1045 Westgate Dr., St. Paul, MN 55114.

Library of Congress Cataloging-in-Publication Data

Cootie shots: theatrical inoculations against bigotry for kids, parents and teachers /
edited by Norma Bowles.—1st ed.
        p.cm
      Includes bibliographical references.
      ISBN 1-55936-184-0 (alk. Paper)
        1. Children's plays, American. 2. Toleration—Juvenile
        drama. 3. Difference (Psychology)—Juvenile drama.
        4. Pluralism (Social Sciences)—Juvenile drama.
        [1. Prejudices—Drama. 2. Individuality—Drama. 3. Plays.]
        I. Bowles, Norma.

PS625.5 C66 2000
812'.60809282—dc21   00-037758

Front cover (clockwise from top right): illustration by Christopher Myers, photograph by Kathi Kent and drawing by Suk Gyu Sean Kim.

Back cover: Lynn Capri's 4th and 5th Grade Leaders, Foundations School Community.

Book, design and composition by 2^b Group Inc.

COOTIE SHOTS

is dedicated to all of us:

to everyone who has ever been hurt by cruel words, actions or inactions;

to everyone who has ever hurt others with cruel words, actions or inactions;

and to everyone who has ever helped others by speaking out, standing up and getting involved!

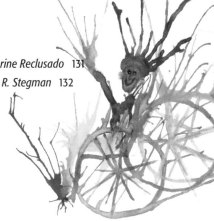

ACKNOWLEDGMENTS

Fringe Benefits is indebted to so many thoughtful and generous people whose contributions of time, energy, hard work, ideas, stories, talent, food, space and funds have made *Cootie Shots* possible.

First and foremost, we want to thank the more than five hundred youth, educators, parents, artists, therapists and social workers who graciously donated their writings, artwork and ideas to *Cootie Shots*.

For their good humor and tireless work to make this book sing, much thanks to the fabulous designer, Bob Stern, and the entire staff at Theatre Communications Group, especially Terry Nemeth, Kathy Sova and Leigh Zona. We thank Rosa Furumoto for her support and thoughtful preface.

We also wish to extend our heartfelt thanks to the foundations and organizations whose generous financial contributions made *Cootie Shots* possible. Extra special thanks to the Liberty Hill Foundation, for believing in us early on and for continuing to help us grow and flourish. Special thanks to: California Community Foundation Brody Arts Fund, Joseph Drown Foundation, Entertainment Industry Foundation, GLSEN/L.A., The Kolla-Landwehr Foundation, Lesbian and Gay Community Fund, Liberty Hill Foundation/Richard and Stacy Beale Fund, Liberty Hill Foundation/Fund for Progressive Change, Liberty Hill Foundation/Joseph B. Kirshbaum Memorial Fund, Liberty Hill Foundation/Leff-Donahue Family Fund, Liberty Hill Foundation/Rhino Records Fund, The Los Angeles Gay and Lesbian Center and Threshold Foundation.

Norma Bowles wishes to dedicate her work on *Cootie Shots* to two extraordinary people: Norma Bowles, Sr.–Mom!–a wise, gutsy, loving and lovable gal, and Lynn Bielefelt, a truly inspirational teacher, conductor and human being.

There are so many wonderful people to thank for their commitment to and assistance with this project and the work of Fringe Benefits that we have devoted a full acknowledgments section to them at the back of this book. We thank you all.

PREFACE
Rosa Furumoto

From the moment I first worked with Norma Bowles, I thought, This woman is insane! I soon learned that Norma's particular brand of madness can spark joy, love, tears, acceptance, laughter, reflection and positive change in communities. Without a doubt she is an irrepressible and inimitable teacher, visionary, performer, author and theatre activist with a deep sense of commitment to making the world a more accepting place for all people. As the Founder and Artistic Director of Fringe Benefits, a Los Angeles-based educational theatre company, Norma has inspired the development of an amazing collection of plays, songs and interactive performance pieces against bigotry by a coalition of elementary school teachers, parents, theatre artists, therapists, administrators and students.

The *Cootie Shots* performance pieces contain powerful messages against discrimination and intolerance based on race, class, gender, sexual orientation, religion and physical ability. The plays encourage children, young adults and adults to work against name-calling, bullying and other acts of violence in their schools, homes and neighborhoods. Through the use of funny songs, mirthful music and lively characters, one is drawn in to understand and care about the characters' dilemmas. While driven to laughter, one sees himself/herself reflected back, and realizes, Hey, that could be me! or What would I do in a similar situation?

The *Cootie Shots* plays are not simply the work of theatrical writers, but rather that of passionately engaged theatre activists and other members of the community. Through all the plays and songs runs a common thread of people committed to justice, respect and human dignity. In this sense, *Cootie Shots* is like a collective sociopolitical record of important issues facing our schools and communities. Almost every play contains elements of humor, idealism and hope for the future. *The Golden Rule* addresses intolerance toward religion by including four young characters: a Sikh, a Jew, a Catholic and an agnostic or atheist. The result is a highly engaging, entertaining and informative performance that gets the audience to laugh and think about our quickness to judge the religious behavior of others.

The War of the Stuck-up Noses challenges class discrimination. Here, we find a school girl willing to take a stand for a new girl mistreated because of her mismatched, brightly colored clothing purchased at a discount store. The play leaves the audience with practical ideas about how to counteract class discrimination among their friends. It also makes a statement about human decency and standing up for justice.

The ordinary settings of schools and playgrounds make the plays all the more meaningful to children. *Anyone for Double Dutch?* examines the institutionalized gender stereotyping associated with sports played at school. Children have to stop and think about what they are doing when they say, "Only sissies jump rope."

The *Cootie Shots* performances have created powerful ripples in numerous communities and schools. I want to share with you an example of the power of these plays and songs to inspire and transform a community's attitudes, views and behavior. The Fringe Benefits theatre company had been invited to perform the *Cootie Shots* plays for an auditorium filled with our elementary students. We invited some parent leaders from two local schools to watch the performance and give us their feedback. The *Cootie Shots* performance delighted the children, and the dialogue that Norma led throughout truly engaged the children. They asked questions about the plays and discussed their concerns about name-calling, sissy-baiting and bullying on our elementary school campus.

As we walked away from the auditorium, I wondered how the Latina parent leaders would react to the *Cootie Shots* performance. Although these parent leaders had already demonstrated that they were concerned about racism and other forms of discrimination, I wasn't sure how they would react to the play *Doing the Right Thing*, about a Latino, homosexual young man and his younger sister. Homosexuality is a highly sensitive issue in this overwhelmingly Catholic Latino community, but the parents unanimously responded by saying: "We want them to perform *Cootie Shots* for the parents at our

ix

next parent multicultural training session." At the time I didn't realize that these parents would soon be trailblazing with Norma at the helm.

These parents were also inspired by *All the Adams in the World*, which addresses discrimination against those with different abilities. And they were intrigued by the message about gender stereotyping in *Rapunzel*. The message that long hair is a form of control over girls and women to assure "gender appropriate" behavior resonated with the mothers. With *Four Heroes* they felt a great sense of inclusion because it included Cesar Chavez as well as Dr. Martin Luther King, Jr. and Rosa Parks. They insisted that other parents needed to see these plays so that they could teach their children about respect and understanding.

Cootie Shots was performed for about forty Latina parents from our two elementary schools. I was stunned by the reaction of the parents. Something about the plays struck a sympathetic chord with these Latina mothers. Not only did they love the plays, they insisted that they wanted to create their own play(s) to address gender stereotyping, machismo and homophobia in the Latino community. Norma has made this happen time and time again with the help of other committed members of the artistic community.

The Latina parents started talking to their children and other family members about gender stereotyping in the families. They discussed their responsibility in perpetuating the lower status of girls and women in Latino homes and in the community. The question of how we treat homosexuals was openly discussed for the first time and the parents began encouraging tolerance and understanding with their family members. In some cases the victories have been seemingly small, as in allowing their daughters to go away to college instead of insisting that they stay close to home. The important first step is acknowledging that change in our community is necessary.

Our students have also taken important steps toward internalizing the messages of the *Cootie Shots* plays. Parents and teachers have followed up the *Cootie Shots* plays by encouraging children to stand up to name-calling and sissy-baiting and to "do the right thing" when they see injustice in their school. We have seen a significant reduction in the incidence of violence and name-calling in our school community, and an increase in respectful behavior among children and between children and adults.

The struggle against injustice, intolerance, discrimination and violence is truly a struggle for our humanity. Each of us carries the seeds of possibility and hope for a better world. The beauty and power of *Cootie Shots* is that it encourages young people and adults to consider a different kind of world in which each of us can be a hero or heroine who stands up to injustice the way Rosa Parks did. The plays empower us to face our fears and shame about who we are and to recognize how we mistreat our fellow human beings. And as the plays and songs unfold, one realizes that we are all performers on a stage and that every one of us can choose to be the heroine or hero of kindness and justice or the perpetrator of pain and intolerance.

Here, at last, for all our benefit—in all its trailblazing glory—is the incredible, delightful and life-changing *Cootie Shots*!

June 2001, Los Angeles

Rosa Furumoto is a multicultural trainer and director for the school-based Every Child A Learner Project in Pacoima, CA, and a faculty advisor with the UCLA Center X Teacher Education Program.

INTRODUCTION

Cootie Shots is a book about words—powerful words that can both hurt and heal. It is designed to teach children that they have a choice about the words they use, and that they have the power to change their world through their words.

Cootie Shots was created by Fringe Benefits, a Los Angeles-based educational theatre company, in collaboration with more than 500 elementary school teachers, parents, therapists, administrators, theatre artists, visual artists and youth. Since 1991, Fringe Benefits has been helping children enter into constructive dialogue on issues of tolerance and diversity. Fringe Benefits has presented over 100 performances of *Cootie Shots*, most of them in elementary schools throughout California, reaching over 20,000 youth, parents and teachers.

Cootie Shots is an eclectic mix of plays, songs and poems that promote tolerance, compassion and acceptance. It celebrates diversity by presenting role models of different cultures, ethnicities, classes, genders, abilities, sexual orientations, religions, ages and appearances. The pieces in this book may be performed at home, in the classroom or in a theatre.

These pieces ask children to acknowledge the bigotry and discrimination in their lives, while helping them to imagine and take responsibility for creating a world shaped by love and understanding. By using familiar circumstances, often generated by real-life experiences, these plays assist children in understanding the feelings of everyone affected by cruel words: those who speak them, their targets and their bystanders. By engaging directly with these performance pieces, children learn to honestly and effectively express their feelings. They learn to choose words that heal the hurt and bring people together.

The issues presented here may seem difficult to discuss or even taboo. Yet prejudice and discrimination, though tough topics, are unavoidable ones. Studies show that the effects of discrimination begin to negatively affect children as early as the first grade (even those not directly participating in or targeted by the discrimination).[1] Even 1st graders are now using such terms as "faggot" to ridicule others, and such name-calling is increasingly common in the older grades.[2] Children who are the subject of name-calling and the object of alienation are at a higher risk than others for drug abuse, running away, dropping out, family violence and suicide.[3] Experts agree that these issues are best addressed early in a child's development.[4]

The National Education Association recently stated that: "Discrimination and stereotyping based on such factors as race, gender, immigration status, physical disabilities, ethnicity and sexual orientation must be eliminated. The Association also believes that plans, activities and programs for education of employees, students, parents and the community should be developed to identify and eliminate discrimination and stereotyping in all educational settings."[5]

Similarly, the American Psychological Association stated that: "The American Psychological Association and the National Association of School Psychologists support providing a safe and secure educational atmosphere in which all youths, including lesbian, gay and bisexual youths, may obtain an education free from discrimination, harassment, violence and abuse, and which promotes an understanding and acceptance of self."[6]

Cootie Shots is a ground-breaking program created "to eliminate discrimination in educational settings" and to help "promote an understanding and acceptance of self."

Fringe Benefits works "within a collaborative frame whereby contributors use their own stories to generate understanding and compassion, to generate sociopolitical activism, to dismantle the conventional theatrical frame and to de-essentialize cultural and gender identities."[7] Many of the pieces in this book were born of a group of people in a room, collaborating to turn painful stories into theatre that heals that pain, or, better still, prevents future injuries. Each person added to the mix, whether through writing or improvising or by offering suggestions.

This is how a typical play development session works:

Two mothers offer to host a playmaking session. A diverse group of about two dozen people gathers to brainstorm, write and improvise. There's a thirteen-year-old girl and her mom, some teachers, a Catholic priest, a rabbinical student, a family of four, several therapists, a number of playwrights and actors, several formerly homeless youth, the hosts, a grandmother and a toddler. All share a common goal: we all want to find creative ways to address the rise of hate crimes among youth.

The session begins with a question. "What's the scariest thing you or your child had to face in elementary school?" A girl tells of how she was tortured because she was overweight, another girl because of her speech impediment. A mother and father tell how both their son and daughter are harassed because their son is gay. A young man tells how he heard snickers when his recognizably Jewish name was called each day in class. One of the formerly homeless youth describes the place where he hid during recess to get away from the kids calling him "indio," "blackie" and "nigger."

Then the improvisations begin. Adults play children, teenagers play teachers, as the stories are acted out and recorded for later transcription and refinement. Everyone has crucial input: "But that isn't how a ten-year-old boy would really react." "Try this, it'll make it

funnier." "That really fits with our school's philosophy." "That made me cry." "You won't be allowed to say that in a school setting, but that's what's really going on."

This scenario is repeated many times, in over sixty workshops held in various homes, classrooms and youth shelters, with dozens of different participants. Each week new issues and new stories are explored through discussion and improvisation.

In a workshop that Fringe Benefits conducted with members of Parents, Families and Friends of Lesbians and Gays/L.A. (PFLAG/LA), after they saw our high school show, *Turn It Around!,* the Gutierrez Family shared their experiences dealing with the discrimination their daughter was facing in school. In subsequent workshops they offered constructive feedback as their story was gradually developed through improvisation, then shaped by Cynthia Ruffin, into the pithy short play, *Doing the Right Thing.* Sometimes, the workshops served a double purpose, allowing the Gutierrez Family, and other participants, an opportunity to rehearse how they might deal with future real-life situations, such as a meeting with the principal. When we perform *Doing the Right Thing*, we find that the piece resonates with people in many different ways. When the actress playing Tonia asks the children in the audience if they've "ever been called a name that isn't very nice," the response is an almost unanimous: "Yes!" Nearly a third of the children tell us that that the name-calling hurts so much that they, like Tonia, have wanted to change schools to try to escape it. Many children offer wonderful suggestions about what to do when their friends start bullying someone the way Tonia was bullied. And many, many children, parents and teachers tell us how helpful it is to see this issue presented in such an open and constructive manner.

In all, twelve imaginative and thought-provoking pieces included in *Cootie Shots* emerged from workshops: they were either generated from the seed of an idea during a brainstorming session or developed through improvisation and then formalized into a play. Many inspiring pieces in this collection were created by individual artists and educators who were eager to lend their voice to the project. Other pieces in the book were written before *Cootie Shots* was conceived, the artists graciously allowing us to include their work in this anthology. Some pieces were adapted from existing longer works, either by the artists themselves, in collaboration with Fringe Benefits, or by Fringe Benefits with the artists' permission. For instance, Chris Wells waved his magic wand over his full-length one-man show *Liberty!* and turned it into the delightful monologue included in this book. And the reactions of audiences to *Cootie Shots* have been very gratifying. A number of people have seen the show and then asked if they could write, develop or illustrate something for the book. After a performance at Highways Performance Space, for example, Joseph Brouillette, asked if he could write a piece based on a friendship he had with a deaf boy when he was young. The result is the heartwarming play, *Shy Kevin and Curious Joe*.

Similarly, the artwork that illustrates and decorates *Cootie Shots* was contributed by a wide variety of artists. Many stunning pieces were created expressly for the anthology. We found many of the talented artists in much the same way as we found the contributing writers: by reputation, by the recommendations of the writers, through friends and through friends of friends. Artist Rose Portillo, for example, was a natural for *The Other Side of the Fence*, as she has transformed her home here in Los Angeles into a work of art, a kind of year-round *Dias de los Muertos* altar. Some artwork came with the piece it illustrates, such as Lynette Schmidt's drawings for *The Duke Who Outlawed Jelly Beans*, which appear in the children's book from which our short play is adapted. Production and archival photos as well as candid snapshots are also used. And, once again, the audience got into the act: children who saw the show at their elementary schools sent in drawings, along with thoughtful comments. Hundreds and hundreds of colorful, imaginative drawings were sent to us, and many are used here. And, last but not least, extraordinary existing artwork was also contributed to the book by a number of artists or their estates. We are particularly grateful to have the beautiful artwork for *Given All I've Got* and *La Peluca de Su Mama*, which was contributed by the family of San Francisco artist and dear friend, Dan Bielefelt, who passed away in May 2000. And we are grateful to Scholastic Press for their generous contribution of artwork to *That Race Place*, *Ode to Parents* and *Shy Kevin and Curious Joe*.

When we began work on *Cootie Shots*, back in 1998, we had no idea how much wonderful material (plays and artwork) would emerge. With so many talented writers and artists participating in this project, the task of selecting only fifty-four pieces for this anthology was quite challenging. We regret that we couldn't include all the fabulous artwork and writing that was contributed. We owe a huge debt of gratitude to all the writers and artists, youth, parents, teachers, therapists, administrators, activists and actors who collaborated with us to make *Cootie Shots*. Whether their names are attached to a specific piece or not, their wisdom, humor and passion are woven into the fabric of this anthology. *Cootie Shots* would not have been possible without the invaluable contributions of *everyone* involved. When you read our acknowledgments sections and Artists Biographies, you will see that it took a village to create this book. Here's hoping you will assemble your own village, and share your words with a world that sorely needs them! *Cootie Shots* is about people finding their own true, unique and powerful voices and using those voices to change the world. Spread the word.

Norma Bowles, Editor
Mark E. Rosenthal, Associate Editor
Los Angeles, June 2001

[1] Lenore Gordon, "Rethinking Our Classroom," *The Bulletin of the Council on Interracial Books for Children* 14 (3 & 4).

[2] Ibid.

[3] Websites:
The Massachusetts Department of Education: www.doe.mass.edu
GLSEN: www.glsen.org
PFLAG: www.pflag.org

[4] Resolution on Lesbian, Gay and Bisexual Youths in the Schools, adopted by the American Psychological Association Council of Representatives on February 28, 1993, and by the National Association of School Psychologists on January 16, 1993.

[5] National Education Association 1998–99 Resolutions, B-8, Racism, Sexism and Sexual Orientation Discrimination.

[6] Same as footnote 4.

[7] Amadeu J. Pavini, "Fringe Benefits Theatre," paper presented at the Room for Play: Drama, Theatre and Performativity Conference, University of Southern California, February 24, 2001.

MY FAMILY TREE

IS A GARDEN!

Art by Lauren Yoshikawa, Clover Avenue Elementary, 4th Grade

MY FAMILY TREE ...

Ms. Langley's 1st Grade Leaders, Thirty-Second Street Visual and Performing Arts/Math/Science/ Technology, Los Angeles
Bottom row (left to right): Candice Cho; James Robinson; Lauren Cannell; Aneiki Randolph; Roxanne Flores; Daniel Martin. Middle row: Heela Kang; Dennis Argueta; Anna Brancaccio; Antoine Louis, Jr.; Leslie Guzman; Meshach Puerto. Top row: Barbara Silva; Arianna Sanchez; Justina Lee; Marlene Briones; Sharon Cespedes. Emma Benitez (teaching assistant) is top left and Sharon Langley (teacher) is top right

I like my friend
His name is Tiger
He is not my blood, but I love him.

I love my cousin Gordon
He is not my cousin
But, I still love him
And it feels like he is my cousin
And I even know how old he is
He is fourteen.

I love my mom and dad because
They are very, very nice moms and dads
Sometimes they are not home
I still love them.

I have another sister
She is eleven years old
We met in Korea
She's my mom's friend's daughter
She is my friend
I like my sister
Katherine always says, "Let's go play outside!"
I like to play with her
When I'm sad, she says, "Do you want a glass of water?"
And I feel happy.

My auntie's friend is my friend too.
His name is Michael.
Michael almost always says, "Hey."
I feel Michael is part of my family.

I love my brother Joey because he
Is very nice to me
And sometimes he tickles me
He is my dad's son
And Joey also has another brother
And sister
And this makes five kids.

I have a friend
Her name is Anell
She is skinny and she is
My aunt
She is a big girl
I like to play tic-tac-toe
With her
We are good friends.

I love my sister and her name is Anita
My sister wears glasses because she watches TV too much
My sister bends her back because her backpack is heavy
I hug my sister and my sister loves me
I love my sister
So
So
So
Much.

by Ms. Langley's 1st Grade Leaders

Self-portrait collages are by (clockwise from the top): Arianna Sanchez, Meshach Puerto, Daniel Martin, Justina Lee

My daddy is
my family.

I have a cousin and her name is Naomi
My mom was friends with Naomi's mom when they were little
They are still friends
I call her Naomi-Oni, that means "sister" in Korean
Sometimes, Naomi-Oni tickles me and says, "Goochie, goochie, goo!"
And I say, *"Stop,"* in a quiet voice and she stops
And I feel happy.

I love my dad because he loves me too.

My friend Ivan is like a big brother to me
When I finish lunch, I play with him
We go to see the ants because we like them
We feed them seeds from the house
It takes ten ants to carry one sunflower seed.

... IS A GARDEN!

My other mom's name is Sharon
She has a big hat, big hair, big socks and little shoes
My other mom likes to jump with me.

The person who looks like my sister
But isn't in my family
Is Tiara.

My dad is not part of my family
My dad is dark black
And looks like a car
And walks and sounds like a killer elephant
My dad is funny
I like to wrestle with my daddy
I get him in a pedigree!

My uncle's name is Gerardo
My aunt married him
I love him because he is nice to me
He likes to make the *Flintstones* voices
He says, "Wilma, I'm home!"
He tells jokes and acts like a clown
And his jokes are funny
He is funny too!

I like my auntie who was
Not born in my family
She cares for me
I love her
She loves me also.

My brother Bryan is
From another family
But I still love him
He came to my family because his dad and my
Mom got married
Because they loved and cared for each other
He always calls me an elephant to make me laugh
Yesterday, he said,
"Truth or Dare?"
I said, "Truth."
Then he said, "Is it true that you are an elephant?"
I said, "No."
Bryan said, "Yes, you are because you said, 'Truth'!"

WHAT COLOR IS YOUR MAMA?

by Carol S. Lashof

Based on a true story by Shevra Tait and her daughter, Dina Tait Barker

Very special thanks to kindergarten teacher, Amy Morton, and her students at Washington Elementary School in Berkeley

4

Art by Madison Wells Kimbro, Crossroads School, 3rd Grade

Ms. TAYLOR stands in front of her classroom holding a sheaf of construction paper ranging in colors from cream to ebony. BRIANA and CHARLES sit next to each other. RICKY is nearby.

MS. TAYLOR   I'm going to come around with the paper and you can choose which color you want to use for your self-portrait. Now, you're not going to find a piece of paper that exactly matches your skin color because I only have about ten different colors here. And how many different colors of skin do you think there are in the world?

BRIANA   A thousand!

CHARLES   A million!

RICKY   A katillion and one!!

MS. TAYLOR   There are twenty-two people in this classroom. And I bet none of us has exactly the same skin color.

(The children begin holding hands up next to each other to compare. Meanwhile, Ms. TAYLOR is handing out pieces of paper.)

BRIANA   *(to CHARLES)* I'm darker than you are.

RICKY   *(to Ms. TAYLOR)* Do you have peachy gold?

BRIANA   *(to CHARLES)* Who was that lady that picked you up yesterday?

CHARLES   What lady?

BRIANA   The lady that picked you up.

CHARLES   My mommy picked me up. She always picks me up. Except sometimes my daddy, or if I'm going over to my friend's house–

BRIANA   Was that your friend's mama?

CHARLES   Who?

BRIANA   *(loudly)* The lady who picked you up!

CHARLES   *(confused)* My mom picked me up.

BRIANA   *(definite)* That was not your mama!

CHARLES   *(upset)* It was too my mama!

BRIANA   What color is your mama?

(Ms. TAYLOR arrives at CHARLES and BRIANA's table with the sheaf of paper. She has heard the last exchange and sees that CHARLES is at a loss for words.)

MS. TAYLOR   Briana, are you thinking that Charles couldn't have a light-skinned mother?

BRIANA   Well, yeah. His mama can't be white, can she?

MS. TAYLOR   Why not?

BRIANA   Well, 'cuz when you have a baby … I mean, 'cuz Charles is black and …

RICKY   Maybe his daddy is black.

BRIANA   Is your daddy black, Charles?

(CHARLES is silent.)

MS. TAYLOR   Maybe if you ask him nicely, Briana, Charles will tell you about his family. He has a pretty special story to tell.

BRIANA   Is it like a secret?

CHARLES   Uhn-uhn. It's not a secret.

RICKY   You tell us, Ms. Taylor.

MS. TAYLOR   It's up to Charles. It's his story.

(Pause. CHARLES considers. Then to MS. TAYLOR:)

CHARLES   Can I sit in the sharing chair and tell the whole class?

MS. TAYLOR   If you want to.

CHARLES   I do want to.

(MS. TAYLOR and CHARLES walk to the front of the room together. MS. TAYLOR claps a rhythm to get the class's attention: duh-da-da-duh-duh. The class responds: duh-duh.)

MS. TAYLOR   Briana asked Charles some questions about his family. And he's going to answer her questions by telling us all a story. Go ahead, Charles.

CHARLES   Umm. *(pause)* This is my story about my family. *(pause)* By Charles Thomas Olsen. My mommy's name is Ellen Thomas and my daddy's name is Steve Olsen. Before I was born, my mom was very sick. She almost died. But she still wanted to have a baby. And so did my dad. Ellen couldn't have a baby because of being sick. They were very sad 'cuz they really, really wanted a baby. And then they got a great idea. They got the idea to adopt a baby. And that was me! Ellen and Steve are my real mom and dad 'cuz I live with them and they love me and we're a family even though they don't look like me. But I do have another mom and dad, too. Danny and Louise. They're my ... my ... *(CHARLES whispers to MS. TAYLOR, then turns back to the class)* They're my biological parents. That means they borned me. 'Cuz everybody's gotta get borned. One time, I asked my mom and dad why Danny and Louise didn't want to keep me and my dad said it wasn't about that, it was about could they be a good mom and dad or not. And they decided not, 'cuz they were too young and a lot of other stuff and they wanted me to have a mom and dad who were really, really ready to be a mom and dad, and so they picked my mom and dad to be my mom and dad and ... and that's how I got my family ... the end.

MS. TAYLOR   Thank you, Charles. That was a wonderful story. Is it okay if the class asks you questions?

(CHARLES nods. Hands are immediately raised.)

CHARLES   *(teacherly)* Yes, Ricky.

RICKY   Ms. Taylor, can I tell a family story, too?

MS. TAYLOR   Not today because we have to finish our self-portraits, but tomorrow you can. Does anyone have a question for Charles? *(pause)* Yes, Briana.

BRIANA   Who picked your name? Was it your mom and dad or was it Danny and Louise?

CHARLES   Well, when I was about to be born, Steve and Ellen went to the hospital. And they were there when I was born and they had some different ideas for names but they wanted Louise to help choose 'cuz, well, they just thought it was more fair. And she liked Charles because she had an Uncle Charles and also my dad liked it 'cuz his grandpa's name was Charles. So, I'm Charles. *(pause)* And if you want to know, Danny and Louise don't live near me but I have pictures of them and Danny is ... *(he looks through the stack of paper and chooses a dark brown sheet)* ... about this color and Louise is this color *(chooses a cream-colored sheet)* and that's why I look like this.

(CHARLES sorts through the paper until he finds one that comes close to matching his skin color. He holds it up next to his face.)

BRIANA	Like _____! *(fill in the kind of coffee—with or without cream—that most closely matches the skin color of the actor)* That's how my daddy drinks his coffee. Ms. Taylor, can my daddy come to school next week and tell stories? He tells good stories.
MS. TAYLOR	Sure. That would be great, Briana.
RICKY	Can my mom come?
MS. TAYLOR	Everybody's mom or dad can come. Or their aunt or uncle or grandpa or big sister … just not all on the same day. Right now, though, I think we'd better work on our self-portraits. It'll be lunchtime in ten minutes.
BRIANA	Families are like skin color, huh, Ms. Taylor?
MS. TAYLOR	How?
CHARLES	I know. Because there are all different colors of skin …
MS. TAYLOR	Oh! Yes … and there are all different kinds of families, too. Is that what you meant, Briana?
BRIANA	Yeah. Thousands!
CHARLES	Millions!
RICKY	A katillion and one!

Art by Lynette Schmidt

THE DUKE WHO OUTLAWED JELLY BEANS

by Johnny Valentine
Stage adaptation by Norma Bowles

This play may be performed with four to twenty-four actors. This piece is best staged with a lot of action. For example, the NARRATOR should act out the story rather than just narrate it. A no-holds-barred approach is best.

NARRATOR   The kingdom was ruled by a king and queen, who one day called all of their subjects to hear a proclamation.

(The NARRATOR, with a mask, plays the KING, while the QUEEN, another actor with a mask, stands at his side.)

KING   Hear ye, hear ye!

Narrator   Announced the king from the castle balcony.

KING   The queen and I must go away for many months to visit the Kingdom of Asphodel. While we are away, our nephew, the Grand Duke Archibald, will rule the kingdom.

NARRATOR   With that, the king and queen climbed into their coach, pulled by six beautiful white horses, and rode away. Immediately the Grand Duke Archibald strode out on the balcony.

(Again, the NARRATOR, with a mask, plays the DUKE.)

DUKE   Hear ye, hear ye!

NARRATOR   He called out, puffing up his chest. He sounded funny, as if he were holding his nose while he talked.

DUKE   I have a decree to issue. *(pauses, then scratches his head)* My decree is … uh … that everyone must come back tomorrow to hear my next decree!

ANNA   That's the stupidest decree I ever heard.

NARRATOR   Declared Anna, a young girl who was in the crowd along with her parents.

JUDITH   He probably just couldn't think of anything else—

NARRATOR   Explained Judith, her mother.

JUDITH   Give him time. He's new at this.

ANNA   Doesn't he know how silly he sounds?

MARIAN   I think he's pretending to have an accent—

NARRATOR   Explained Marian, her other mother.

MARIAN   Some people do that to feel more important.

NARRATOR   The next day, everyone returned. The Grand Duke Archibald strutted out on the balcony and puffed up his chest.

DUKE   Hear ye, hear ye: I proclaim that too many jelly beans are being eaten. We could have a jelly bean shortage if we're not careful. Henceforth, no one shall eat jelly beans without royal permission. I also proclaim that no one may have royal permission.

(Laughter from the crowd.)

    Silence!

NARRATOR   Roared the Grand Duke—

DUKE	I am very serious. Anyone found eating jelly beans shall be beheaded. You will all return in one week for my next proclamation.
NARRATOR	Silently, everyone walked back to their homes. No one ate a single jelly bean. A week later, the Grand Duke Archibald stepped out on the balcony to issue his next decree.
DUKE	Hear ye, hear ye: Today, I proclaim that too many children are being impertinent to their parents. Henceforth, no children shall be allowed to read books that have not received the royal seal of approval! Anyone who disobeys shall lose their head.
ANNA	He's nuts!
MARIAN	I am afraid that doesn't matter. Until the king and queen return, his word is law.
ANNA	What can I do without my books? I'll be bored!
JUDITH	There are other ways to amuse yourself. Why don't you play make-believe?

(ANNA *climbs onto the kitchen table, puffs up her chest, and with her left hand pinches her nose shut. She announces:*)

ANNA	Hear ye, hear ye: I proclaim that anybody who talks like this should have their nose cut off!
MARIAN	(*laughing*) That's very funny, but you mustn't do it in front of anyone else. The Grand Duke wouldn't like being turned into a laughingstock—why, no one would pay him any attention then.

(ANNA *gets a mischievous "that gives me an idea!" look.*)

JUDITH	It's time for bed.
NARRATOR	The next week, the Grand Duke Archibald issued yet another decree.

DUKE	Hear ye, hear ye: Since I grew up with just one mother and one father, and I turned out so well, I proclaim that this arrangement will work best for everyone. In one week any children who have too many mothers or fathers, or not enough, will be thrown into the dungeon.
ANNA	(*whispered*) He can't do that!
MARIAN	(*reaching down to hug* ANNA) I'm afraid he can.
JUDITH	But we'll never let him take you away. We'd flee to another kingdom first.
DUKE	Come back next week for another decree! Oh, and in the meantime, don't forget about the jelly beans!
NARRATOR	That evening after dinner, Anna had an emergency meeting with her friend Peter. They made a list.
PETER	There's Nicholas. He has two dads. That's one dad too many, according to the Grand Duke!
ANNA	And don't forget his new brother Jesse!
PETER	And Gaston lives with his grandparents!
ANNA	What about Scarlett? She just has one mom and no dads. The duke will take her away from her mother, too!
NARRATOR	Soon they had listed twelve other kids who did not have "the right parents" according to the Grand Duke, and who would be taken away from their families. The next day, all the children met secretly in the woods. Anna quickly told them her plan.

The villagers had never seen anything like the week that followed. Children were strutting all about the town, puffing up their chests, holding their noses and making silly speeches. |

ANNA	*(standing on a park bench, puffing up her chest and holding her nose)* Hear ye, hear ye: Henceforth, I proclaim that all pet goldfish must be toilet-trained!
PETER	*(also puffing up his chest, holding his nose, etc.)* Hear ye, hear ye: I proclaim that horses are forbidden to burp!
NICHOLAS	*(also puffing up his chest, holding his nose, etc.)* Hear ye, hear ye: I accidentally swallowed a grasshopper when I was two, and I turned out so well, I proclaim that every two year old must swallow a grasshopper!

(Everyone laughs.)

NARRATOR	Then out strutted the Grand Duke Archibald.
DUKE	*(flustered and freaked-out by the laughter)* Uh … Eh … Ahem … Hear ye, hear ye: I proclaim that giggling is against the law!

(Everyone roars with laughter.)

| DUKE | Guards! *(roaring, his face crimson with embarrassment)* Arrest everyone who's laughing! Off with their heads! |

NARRATOR	But the guards were laughing, too.
GUARD #1	Off with their heads! Off with their noses!
GUARD #2	Send them to bed without any toeses!

(Everyone laughs even harder.)

| NARRATOR | The Grand Duke had never been so humiliated in all his life. They were laughing at him!
And so, with his chest still puffed out as far as he could get it, the Grand Duke Archibald strode off the balcony, down the castle stairs and into his coach. He rode out of the kingdom as fast as he could, and he was never seen or heard from again. |
|------|------|
| ANNA | That evening, everyone ate jelly beans for dinner! |
| MARIAN | And except for a few stomachaches that night— |
| JUDITH | They all lived happily ever after. |
| ALL | THE END! |

Altar design and photos by Rose Portillo

THE OTHER SIDE OF THE FENCE

by Jeudi Cornejo Brealey

A couple of days before October 31st. Two adjoining yards of next-door neighbors. On one side of the fence, the Anglo family is busy transforming their backyard into a haunted house for Halloween. On the other side of the fence, the Latino family is busy creating an altar to honor their deceased loved ones for Dias de los Muertos. *Both families are so involved in their own projects that they are oblivious to the sounds coming from the other's yard.*

Once everything is in place, the parents on both sides of the fence return into their respective houses, leaving their ten-year-old children outside. JOEY, *the Anglo child, admires his completed haunted house.* SANDRA, *the Latina child, admires her completed altar. Simultaneously* SANDRA *starts humming a traditional Mexican folk song and* JOEY *turns on his haunted house sound effects. They suddenly become aware of each other.*

JOEY   Sandra?

SANDRA   Yea. Joey?

JOEY   Yea.

SANDRA   What's that screaming?

JOEY   *(playing a prank)* I don't hear anything. *(aside)* This will get her! *(puts on a scary rubber mask)*

SANDRA   Well, it's coming from your yard!

JOEY   If you don't believe me, why don't you come over and have a look yourself. Just crawl under the fence.

(SANDRA crawls under the fence and is met by Joey in his rubber mask.)

SANDRA   *(a little startled, but not scared)* Very funny! What are you supposed to be anyway?

JOEY   A dead guy.

SANDRA   Dead people don't look like that.

JOEY   Yeah, right … like you'd know. *(JOEY removes his mask and sets it on the fence)*

SANDRA   I do.

JOEY   Sure.

SANDRA   *(ignoring his comments)* Wow! What is all this stuff?

JOEY   It's our family's Halloween haunted house. If you'd lived here last year, you'd have remembered it. We make one every fall.

SANDRA   Like a tradition.

JOEY   Yeah.

SANDRA   Sounds like fun!

JOEY   It is! You'll have to see it.

SANDRA   *(wistfully)* I don't usually get to trick-or-treat; my parents think it's too dangerous.

JOEY   Yeah, that's why my parents started this. Now, it's turned into a huge block party and all the families come! We have a costume contest, bob for apples, carve pumpkins and then we have a big potluck dinner!

SANDRA   Sounds great! *(picking up a can of Silly String)* What do you use this for?

JOEY   Oh! This year we're making a giant spider web and whoever plays the spider gets to spray everyone with this stuff.

(He opens the can and sprays SANDRA. She runs. He chases her. She picks up another can and it becomes a Silly String war. Tired, they both collapse laughing.)

JOEY   My whole family dresses up like ghosts and spirits and dead zombies and ghouls, and then we jump out at people and scare them.

SANDRA   *(teasing)* And they're scared of you!?

JOEY   You just wait and see, you'll be scared, too. *(pause)* Are you going to be anything for Halloween?

SANDRA   I dunno yet, but I am going to be a *calavera* for *Dias de los Muertos*.

JOEY   Huh?

SANDRA   I dress like a skeleton on *Days of the Dead*.

JOEY	What's that?	SANDRA	Sometimes there are neighborhood parades and we kids dress up in costumes like—
SANDRA	It's when we honor our family members who have passed … the dead relatives. We celebrate their lives and invite their spirits to visit us again.	JOEY	Like skeletons right?

JOEY   What's that?

SANDRA   It's when we honor our family members who have passed … the dead relatives. We celebrate their lives and invite their spirits to visit us again.

JOEY   *(getting a little scared)* Hey, Sandra … have you really seen dead people?

SANDRA   *(stretching the truth)* Of course.

(A scary sound effect scream is heard. JOEY jumps, then sees his own mask, and jumps again. SANDRA laughs. JOEY turns off the recording.)

SANDRA   Hey, let's crawl over to my yard and you can see how we celebrate—

JOEY   *(sarcastically)* Dead people?

SANDRA   Yes, dead people, and dead pets, too.

JOEY   I think I better stay here. I'm allergic to cats.

SANDRA   Joey, there's nothing to be afraid of. It's just like my grandmother says: "It's not the dead we should be afraid of; it's the living." Yep, *Abuelita* says death's just part of a cycle, like plants have, and that's why we celebrate at harvest time. Look, I'll show you our altar and you'll see …

(She takes him by the hand, and reluctantly he crawls under the fence with her. A beautifully decorated altar stands before them. Placed on it are photos of loved ones, bouquets of marigolds, personal belongings and a variety of skeletal figures.)

JOEY   Wow! I've never seen anything like this! Spooky! Are you in a cult or something?

SANDRA   No, I'm not in "a cult or something"! Lots of people celebrate the dead … people all over the world have different traditions with different names. In some places, it's called *All Soul's Day* or *All Hallow's Eve*. In the U.S., *All Hallow's Eve* has turned into the scary day called *Halloween*, but in my culture, even though it's called *Days of the Dead*, there's nothing spooky about it! It's fun! And in most places, it lasts three whole days!

JOEY   Yeah?!

SANDRA   Sometimes there are neighborhood parades and we kids dress up in costumes like—

JOEY   Like skeletons right?

SANDRA   Yep! And we go to the cemetery and decorate our relatives' tombstones with bouquets of flowers! *(seeing he's starting to get scared, SANDRA plays on his fears)* In Mexico they even have picnics in the graveyard and stay overnight to keep the spirits company—

JOEY   No way!

SANDRA   *(laughs, ignores him and continues)* But here, you can't do that, so, my family says some prayers and we sing in Spanish and tell stories, and then we come home for a big feast, kind of like Thanksgiving, with special food. Mmmmmm! It's so goooood!

JOEY   *(tentatively)* Sandra … you said before that you invite the spirits to revisit you …

SANDRA   Yeah. I almost forgot! We leave a trail of marigold petals all the way from the cemetery to our house, so the spirits can find us.

JOEY   Aren't you scared?!

SANDRA   No… well, some people believe that the spirits really come home. Maybe they do, but I think it's more like when we remember people who aren't here anymore and tell their stories, it's like they're alive and with us.

JOEY   *(starting to get it)* So, you knew all these people?

SANDRA   Some of them I knew, some of them died before I was born; they're my ancestors. *(points to a photo)* Look, this was my *tata*, my dad's dad. He loved to read, so we put his glasses and a book up here for him as an *ofrenda* or offering. This was my pet dog, Reina, and here's her favorite dog bone. This section is for the children who have died. Most of them died a long time ago, in the days when medicine wasn't very good and things like vaccinations didn't exist. Anyhow, that's why we put out little *calaveras*, skeleton toys, to play with and candy skulls to eat.

JOEY	Geez.	SANDRA	Then you can draw a picture, tell a story, sing a song or even make some food that your Gramps liked and put it here.

JOEY   Geez.

SANDRA   Don't you know anyone who's ever died?

JOEY   Well … my grandpa died when I was really little. And after he died, Grandma got rid of Gramps's stuff 'cuz she said it was too painful to have around. I wish I could have had his glasses or his old fishing hat or something to remember him by.

SANDRA   I'm sorry, Joey. See, that's why we celebrate *Dias de los Muertos*. That way, we'll never forget people. Even ornery old *Tia Rita* gets remembered!

(SANDRA holds up a picture of mean Tia Rita *sneering. They both laugh.)*

JOEY   I sure wish my family would talk about Gramps. I was so little when he died. I try to remember him, but it's like he keeps fading further and further away. I'm afraid that one day, I won't even be able to remember him at all!

SANDRA   Do you think if we invited your family over, they would celebrate with our family?

JOEY   I don't know … Yeah, if your parents asked, I bet they would. But what if we don't have something special to put up here on the altar?

SANDRA   Then you can draw a picture, tell a story, sing a song or even make some food that your Gramps liked and put it here.

JOEY   I already know what I want to make … one of those fishing flies that he used! I can't wait! But Sandra … do you think Gramps would be upset if I still wore the dead guy rubber mask for Halloween?

SANDRA   Naw, that's just pretend!

JOEY   Hey? You wanna be in our haunted house this year?

SANDRA   That sounds like fun, Joey!

JOEY   I know! Maybe your whole family could be in the haunted house with mine!

SANDRA   Yeah, they'd like that! Ooooh, ooooh! Can I be the spider!

JOEY   Sure! We can share celebrations this year!

SANDRA   Cool! Let's ask our parents!

JOEY   Okay! I can't wait for them to see what's on … *(makes spooky* Twilight Zone *sounds)*

SANDRA and JOEY   … the other side of the fence! Jinx!

(They burst out laughing and run to their houses.)

A DIFFERENT FAMILY

by Michael Kearns

MICHAEL is a man in his late forties. Tia and her friend CASSADY (male or female) are almost five years old. MICHAEL addresses the audience and the children. TIA and CASSADY, unaware of the audience, talk to MICHAEL and each other. At times MICHAEL and TIA's lines overlap; this is indicated by italics.

TIA	My daddy is gay.
CASSADY	Is he purple?
MICHAEL	My daughter is black, I am *white*.
TIA	*White*. And I'm brown.
CASSADY	Are you gay?
TIA	No, my daddy is.
MICHAEL	We've created a family …
CASSADY	Where's your mom?
MICHAEL	… of aunts and uncles, all shapes and sizes. Tia's mother is *sick*.
TIA	*Sick*. She can't take care of me, so my daddy does. I'm four. But, I'm going to be five on my birthday.
MICHAEL	I've had Tia since she was five months old.
CASSADY	I'm almost five. My daddy is not as tall as your daddy.
TIA	My daddy is a jungle gym.
MICHAEL	Adopting Tia was the best thing I've ever done. She's my *friend*.
TIA	*Friend*. He's my friend.
CASSADY	I'm your friend.
MICHAEL	I wanted to be a father more than anything.
CASSADY	You be the mommy. I'll be the baby.
TIA	I'll be the *daddy*!
MICHAEL	*Daddy* is my favorite role to play.
CASSADY	I'll be the mommy.
MICHAEL	And Mommy. I'm Mommy, too.
TIA	Some kids don't have a mommy. Lots.
CASSADY	Does your daddy like girls?
TIA	He likes me …
MICHAEL	I love her *more than anything*!
TIA	*… more than anything*! I love my daddy!
MICHAEL	We're a family.
CASSADY	I like chocolate cookies.
TIA	My daddy says my skin is the color of chocolate.
CASSADY	But your daddy is white.
TIA	Actually, he's vanilla!

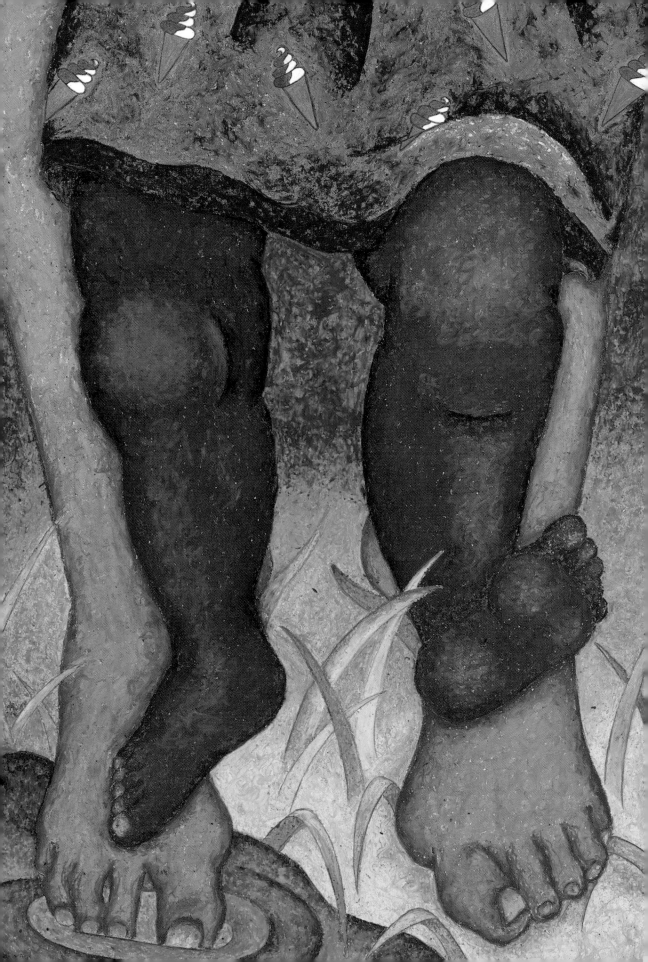

Brittany

My grandmother is my guardian. That means the person who is not my real parent but takes care of me. She gives us a lot of love and kisses and hugs and plays games with us. At my house we do a lot of fun things. Ebony, she likes to play a lot of games, and Gerald always tries to get people in trouble. There are a lot of kids like me, Ebony and Gerald, living with their grandparents, their aunties, and their uncles instead of their parents.

Emily

My name is Emily Fong and I'm in the third grade. My dad's Chinese-American, my mom is German-American. On my dad's side of the family, we celebrate Chinese New Year. From my mom's side we celebrate Christmas. In our family, we have a lot of love, we have a lot of happiness. We have a lot of jokes that make us crack up and fall on the floor laughing … and we have approximately, at least, one fight a day.

THAT'S A FAMILY!

Excerpts from a documentary for kids about family diversity by Debra Chasnoff and Helen S. Cohen

Montana

My name is Montana and I'm in the third grade and my parents are divorced. Divorce is when your parents aren't married anymore, and they move to a different house. Some kids think it's their fault. But don't think that because it's not. It's just that they don't want to be with each other anymore, but it's not your fault. I feel like I have one family, but two houses.

Photos by Debra Chasnoff and Helen S. Cohen

Sam

My parents couldn't have a child and they really wanted one, more than anything, and so they considered something called adoption. Adoption is one of the many ways that you can have a family. When you're adopted, your parents keep you their whole entire life. They don't rent you, they keep you and they love you and they take care of you until you're really big and really old.

Alma

People at my school, they know that my moms are gay, and they know that they love me a lot and they know that we have fun with each other. There's lots of kids that have gay parents and they don't want anyone to know because they think someone's going to make fun of them. Some people might. But some people won't. To have a good family, everyone needs to take care of each other.

Breauna

My name is Breauna and this is my dad, David, and this is my other dad, Greg. My dads are gay, and gay means when two men or two women love each other. It's sort of like having a mom and a dad who love each other. It's just that it's a man and a man, or a woman and a woman. I wish more people understood about being gay and weren't afraid of gay people, and then they wouldn't say mean things about them. If you knew my dads, you would know how cool they are. They're the best dads ever.

Fernando

My name's Fernando. In my family, I only live with one parent. That's my mom. My mom is really, really nice and fun. Whenever I'm in a bad mood or something's wrong, she knows. She gives me a hug and a kiss and asks me, "What's the matter?" I tell her. Then everything just gets better. It doesn't matter who's in the family. But it matters that you love each other and take care of each other. **That's a family.**

LOVE WHAT YOU COOK

by Michele Williams

MAMA (Jewish), stage left, sits at a computer working quietly. DADDY (African-American), stage right, has his toolbox open and is fixing something. We hear a door slam and a girl's voice call out:

KIARA Mama, I'm home! Jasmine's gonna do homework with me!

(Two girls enter: JASMINE, African-American, and KIARA, a relatively light-skinned mix of MAMA and DADDY. Both girls, approximately eleven years old, carry backpacks. They take center stage.)

MAMA *(calls out)* That's fine! She's welcome to stay for dinner.

JASMINE Thanks! I'll call home in a minute and ask.

KIARA Jasmine, y'know if we get this silly food assignment done real quick, we can work on those friendship bracelets before dinnertime.

JASMINE We'll have plenty of time. This food thing—it's so easy! I still don't get it. What does Ms. Jenkins think anyone is going to learn from sharing a menu from our home?

KIARA *(while they get out papers and pencils)* Well, she said something about tracing our cultures … and food being the path. I know it sounds weird … but let's just get it done.

JASMINE All right, close your eyes … It's the weekend, you're hungry, everyone's home and you smell—

KIARA Bacon!

JASMINE That's what I'm talkin' about! How about eggs?

KIARA Make mine over-easy!

JASMINE And—

KIARA and JASMINE *(to the audience)* Grits!

(They turn and face each other.)

JASMINE *(with disbelief)* Your family eats grits!?

KIARA Of course! How else are you gonna eat your eggs?

JASMINE Well, excuuuse me! I guess your daddy's the one cooking the grits.

KIARA Oh, no, my mama's the one. She's probably been eating them all her life. Anyway, why wouldn't she cook them? She cooks the eggs.

JASMINE Well … really, I didn't think white people ate grits.

(The girls walk over to MAMA.)

KIARA Mama?!

MAMA Yes?

Art by Helen Ju

KIARA Mama, haven't you had grits all your life?

MAMA Oh, no! Before your daddy and I got together I didn't know grits from granola!

JASMINE *(to the audience with a smirk)* Unh-huh!

KIARA But you always eat them … and you always cook them!

MAMA Well, it all began because of your daddy. I learned to cook the foods he loves. You remember what I taught you?

KIARA and JASMINE *(facing the audience)* "Cook what you love and you'll love what you cook."

(The girls return to their work.)

JASMINE On to lunch …

KIARA Well, that's easy for me—bagels, cream cheese and lox!

JASMINE I got the bagel. I got the cream cheese … but a lock?

KIARA No, silly! LOX! You know, smoked salmon?

JASMINE I've had breakfast bagels, I've had pizza bagels, but I don't know anything about lox!

KIARA Oh, come on! Doesn't your daddy love lox? My daddy is serious about his! Sometimes he and my Uncle Johnny fight over the last piece! And they're BOTH black!

(Both girls laugh.)

JASMINE *(to the audience)* I don't know about this lox thing … *(to Kiara)* We need your daddy for this one.

(The girls walk over to DADDY.)

KIARA Daddy, what's your favorite fish in the whole, whole world?

DADDY Now, you know the answer to that one—lox! Can you find the needle-nose pliers in there for me?

KIARA *(handing him the pliers)* And you always used to eat it on bagels, like back when you were growing up with Grandaddy and Ma Dear, right?

DADDY Are you kidding? Your mama first took me down there to the bagel shop when I was nineteen, and I've never been the same! If you had brought a bagel in my home growing up, we'd have thought it was a disturbed doughnut!

(The girls walk away.)

KIARA This is harder than I thought!

JASMINE Let's go on to dinner; we're almost done. Let's see … That's easy!

KIARA Mmm … my favorite–take some rice …

JASMINE Throw in some shrimp … a little chicken … lots of seasonings …

KIARA Some all-beef links … and what do you get?

KIARA and JASMINE JAMBALAYA!! *(to the audience)* What do you think? Black? White? Both?

KIARA Now, I know my mama is famous for her jambalaya. I think it might even be somehow Jewish. She made it around Hannukah before. Everybody on both sides comes around when she's cooking it. My Aunt Lena gets her own batch *(in a stage whisper)* before the shrimp go in, of course!

JASMINE (laughing; sarcastically) Well, then, we must be part Jewish, too! Great-Granny in Louisiana makes some screaming jambalaya. We're going to need your mama *and* your daddy for this one!

KIARA (yells) Mama! Daddy! We need you!

(MAMA and DADDY join the girls.)

Jambalaya … (pointing) your family? Or yours? (to JASMINE) Please let this be simple!

JASMINE Amen!

DADDY Well, it goes way back in my family. I've got lots of Louisiana flowing through these veins! But, your mama, she fell in love with jambalaya on her own!

MAMA My mother took me back east to meet some relatives when I was about fifteen. We took the train home and we decided to stop for three days in New Orleans. The food there was the best I've ever had, and I've never stopped cooking my favorite jambalaya since!

MAMA and DADDY Does that answer the question?

KIARA and JASMINE (shaking their heads as all four turn to the audience) Guess the only real answer is …

ALL "COOK WHAT YOU LOVE AND YOU'LL LOVE WHAT YOU COOK!"

"COOK WHAT YOU LOVE AND YOU'LL LOVE WHAT YOU COOK!"

UNCLE CONSTANTIN

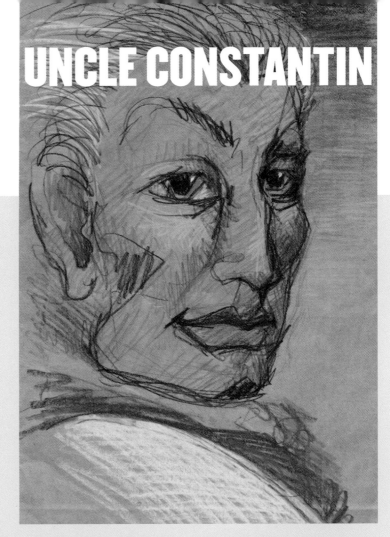

Excerpted from *FAMILY AFFAIRS* by Luis Alfaro

This year Cousin Weenie, who only eats once a day, and Uncle Hector, the cherry-picker, are hosting the *familia* get-together at the home of Weenie's mom, Auntie Esperanza, who has a dinky little place in Fresno. But as Uncle Hector says, "She's got a backyard big enough to kill and cook a pig in."

We hop into the station wagon and head for the Greyhound Bus Station downtown. All of us wear our Sunday best—I even get to wear my favorite clip-on tie, purchased at the Sears on Soto. What's coolest about clip-ons is that, in less than a minute, you can clip that thing on and run in looking like the model son.

After the required egg-throwing contests and three-legged races, like always, I go back to the garden and my aunt's fish pond. I love going to the fish pond because it seems like the only clean place in all of Fresno. Everything in the garden is peaceful.

But the best thing about the garden is that it's where you can always find Uncle Constantin, or "Constance," as my mom calls him. He is always dressed in white, with a scarf around his neck and rings dripping off his fingers. Uncle is the star of our reunions.

Uncle Constantin looks like a movie star. He smells all brand-new, with the scent of the *Tres Flores Brilliantine* holding back his salt-and-pepper hair. You can only see his dark side when he rolls up the sleeves on his white shirt and you notice the markings. Dark blue, like the color of the ocean at night, the designs snake up the inside of his arm and on his fingers.

When he looks down at me—sitting there on the grass, cross-legged, in my clip-on and Sunday suit—he doesn't say anything; he just smiles. Gives me a look. A *look*. Not just any look. The look of *knowing*.

"You and I understand each other, don't we? *Nos entendemos muy bien*." He says it like he looked deep behind my esophagus and found the heart beating under the skinny shell of me.

We look at each other for the longest time, and I get this feeling like when you're at the zoo and you stare at an animal for a long time and you end up seeing a reflection of yourself in that animal.

On the bus ride home, I sit in silence in the last row. I watch as we pass the THANKS FOR VISITING BAKERSFIELD sign and feel a calmness and peace come over me. I know who I am.

Art by Gabrielle Veit-Bermúdez

THE CHILD'S SPIRIT

by Azzam A. Ahmad

The noon sun reached the middle of the clear sky, shining its heat on the calm Kuwaiti water, busy streets, and the open desert. As the shadows disappeared, the mosque towers all over the city chanted the second prayer call that echoed from one neighborhood to the next. It was springtime, the kids had just started their spring break, and it was time to go out camping in the desert. It had been only two decades since this society had switched from the old ways of living to the modern. Despite the physical changes to the city–highways, downtown, modern houses and cars–the society managed to save its old customs, and pass them on to the new generation.

This is where an eight-year-old boy named Azzam lived. *Azzam* is an Arabic word for power. In typical Muslim fashion, Azzam lived with his extended family. He had a powerful bond with his grandmother, *Hussa*, whose name means lesson.

One morning, Azzam ran with excitement from one room to the other to give his grandmother the morning greeting. Following the smell of incense, he found her in the family room, praying. With respect, he slowed down and approached the coal-box where tea and milk containers were being warmed for the expected guests. When his grandmother unbowed from her last kneeling, Azzam realized that she was about to finish praying. He moved closer and sat beside her. At the end of her prayer, she looked over her shoulder and said to his smiling face, "Peace on you and God's mercy!" Then, she did the same to the angel seated on her left shoulder.

Art by C. M. Gross

Azzam stood up, and Hussa said, "Hello, the life of my ancestors! I hope you live a long healthy life!" And she opened her arms and hugged him.

They walked toward the *metrah* (floor mattress) by the coal-box and sat on it. She pulled a tray toward her and asked, "Would you like some warm *haleep* (milk)?"

"Yes," he replied.

She picked up a glass and added two teaspoons of *shakar* (sugar). She grabbed the *haleep* container from the coal-box, and poured the warm *haleep*. With a small spoon she rang into the glass until the *shakar* dissolved. She picked up the *sahan el tamer* (date dish) and said, "Have some *tamer*! Your father's favorite foods when he was a child were *haleep* and *tamer*. Are you ready for the *sahara* (desert) trip this spring break?"

"I love *tamer*, but I am afraid to camp in the *sahara*. There are *hayyaya* (snakes) running around. I learned in school that they bite and we should avoid them."

"You are right, but the *hayyaya* are not as bad as you think. Come and lay down on my lap." She extended her arm and continued, "When I was child I was raised in the *sahara*. We were not afraid of the *hayyaya*, because we were taught how to live *salam* (peacefully) with *hayyawant el sahara* (desert animals)."

Azzam lay down on his back and placed his head on her lap. She combed his hair with her fingers and said, "I will tell you a story of a *hayya* and her lost daughter:

"A long time ago, there was a nomadic family living in the desert. One day, the family had just finished dinner. The mother poured some *haleep* for her children and left the pot by the coal-box where the coal had turned into ashes. Then, she turned off the gaslight, and tucked her children in. While they were asleep, a *hayya* entered the tent and began slivering around the children and the parents. She was looking for her daughter. When she could not find her, she noticed that the family was asleep, and the fire was out, so she assumed that the family had eaten her daughter for dinner. Anger filled her guts as she slivered toward the *haleep* pot. She lifted her head up to the pot's rim and opened her mouth and stuck her fangs to the rim and poisoned the *haleep*. Then, she looked over at the children sleeping on their *metrahs*. She thought of her own daughter. Would causing the deaths of these children bring back her precious child? No. It would not. This act would just spread the pain. She slivered toward the coal-box. She swung her tail onto the box and scooped the ashes from it onto the *haleep*, so the family would not drink from it in the morning. You see, my son, the *hayya* was concerned about her daughter, and really did not want harm for the family.

"With sadness, she left the tent and headed home to her cave. On her way, she found her daughter sound and safe. Her daughter had lost her way home. The mother *hayya* thanked God that she had not let her fear drive out her reason."

"You mean I'm afraid of something that I don't know much about?"

"Yes, your mother had similar feelings when she was a child."

"Really?"

"You know that your mother was born in Yaffa. It was the time when all of us, the Arab Muslims and the Christians, were afraid of the Jews. One day your mother was lost. A Jewish family found her. They brought her to their home. She stayed with them and was treated like their daughter for two weeks while they searched for our family.

"When we finally found her, your mother was no longer afraid of the Jews, and by telling her story, she helped us to conquer our fears as well."

Azzam sat up and gave a kiss to his grandmother and asked, "When are we leaving for the *sahara*."

Grandmother Hussa hugged him close and smiled. "Your father is packing the tent now, and with God's peace, tomorrow morning after the first prayer, we'll drive the car and show you *rooh el sahara* (the desert spirit)!"

PLAY WEDDING

by Christopher Liam Moore

for Emma

NOODLEHEAD's bedroom. NOODLEHEAD and BANANABRAIN, four-year-old girls, play with dolls and stuffed animals. They are both lying on the floor looking up at the ceiling.

BANANABRAIN	And then my brother threw up his Popsicle.
NOODLEHEAD	He's two years old.
BANANABRAIN	He's two, but he sure can throw up a lot of Popsicle.
NOODLEHEAD	I like Popsicles.
BANANABRAIN	I like Popsicles.

(Pause.)

NOODLEHEAD	In the movie, the mermaid has to stop being a mermaid when she gets married.
BANANABRAIN	Why?
NOODLEHEAD	I think because the prince can't live in the ocean.
BANANABRAIN	Oh.

(Pause.)

NOODLEHEAD	Wanna play wedding?
BANANABRAIN	OK.
NOODLEHEAD	I went to a wedding yesterday.
BANANABRAIN	A real wedding?
NOODLEHEAD	A real wedding.
BANANABRAIN	Wow.
NOODLEHEAD	I sang a song with my mother.
BANANABRAIN	At the wedding?
NOODLEHEAD	Yup.
BANANABRAIN	Wow.

(Pause.)

NOODLEHEAD	OK. Let's make Mr. Lizard and the Gorilla get married.
BANANABRAIN	No. Let's make Mr. Lizard and Barbie get married.
NOODLEHEAD	No. Mr. Lizard and the Gorilla.
BANANABRAIN	But, Noodlehead, they can't get married.
NOODLEHEAD	Yes, they can, Bananabrain.
BANANABRAIN	No, they can't.
NOODLEHEAD	Why?
BANANABRAIN	Because they're boys.
NOODLEHEAD	So?

BANANABRAIN	Mr. Lizard is a boy and the Gorilla is a boy. Two boys can't have a wedding.
NOODLEHEAD	That's not true.
BANANABRAIN	Yes it is.

(Pause.)

NOODLEHEAD	The wedding yesterday was two boys.

(Pause.)

BANANABRAIN	Who are the boys who had the wedding?
NOODLEHEAD	My Uncle Chester and his boyfriend.
BANANABRAIN	They really had a wedding?
NOODLEHEAD	Yes, they really, really had a wedding. And I sang a song with my mother. I was scared to sing.
BANANABRAIN	Did they wear dresses?
NOODLEHEAD	No, they had ties.
BANANABRAIN	Did they have flowers?
NOODLEHEAD	Yup. And I had flowers in my hair.
BANANABRAIN	Did they kiss?
NOODLEHEAD	Yup. For a long time.

(Pause.)

BANANABRAIN	What did it look like?
NOODLEHEAD	What?
BANANABRAIN	When they kissed.
NOODLEHEAD	I don't know.
BANANABRAIN	How do two boys kiss?
NOODLEHEAD	I don't know. It looked like when my mommy and daddy kiss. The same thing. Then, after they kissed, everybody clapped.
BANANABRAIN	Wow.

(Pause.)

NOODLEHEAD	So can we make Mr. Lizard and the Gorilla get married now?
BANANABRAIN	OK. But then we have to make them kiss.
NOODLEHEAD	OK.
BANANABRAIN	Because boys can have a wedding.
NOODLEHEAD	Yup. My Uncle Chester did.
BANANABRAIN	And boys can kiss boys when they have a wedding.
NOODLEHEAD	Yup. My Uncle Chester did. For a long time.
BANANABRAIN	OK. I wanna be the Gorilla.
NOODLEHEAD	I think I wanna be the Gorilla.
BANANABRAIN	OK.
NOODLEHEAD	Did your brother really throw up a Popsicle?
BANANABRAIN	Yup. And it was the purple flavor.
NOODLEHEAD	Wow.

(They start to play wedding with Mr. Lizard and the Gorilla. Lights fade.)

BIG LOVE

by Mark E. Rosenthal

My dad and my mom are both different races,
Which means that they don't have the same color faces.
My mom's face is as dark as a warm summer's night,
And my dad's face is seven shades whiter than white.
I'm in the middle of both, sorta tannish;
Lots of folks meet me and start speaking Spanish.
Good thing my uncle's from Mexico City,
He's taught me some words, like *bonita* means pretty.
Mi familia's my family; *gran amor*'s big love!
These are two of the things I am most certain of!

Dad moved away from us when I was five,
So my mom's had to teach me the ways to survive.
She's pretty strong, she does not need a man,
'Cuz anything men can do, my mother can!
She can fix the car's engine while whipping up dinner,
With enough time to still make me feel like a winner.
She's taught me to help out by doing my chores,
In the yard we go camping with cocoa and s'mores.
She's a nurse in real life, so to my bruises she tends,
We're more than just mother and son, we're best friends!

On Mondays through Thursdays, Mom tucks me in bed,
But on weekends and summers, Dad does it instead.
They don't live together but they do still love me,
And now there's more branches on our family tree.
Dad's new wife is Sandy and her son is Ramon.
I just got a new brother and he's fully grown!
Mom's husband is Larry, I went to their wedding—
His cat is now our cat and she needs lots of petting.
My mom helps me with math, that's her special mom zone,
When I stay with my dad, Mom helps over the phone.
My dad loves to read, I love a good story.
And his stories rock! They're wild and gory!

I used to wish they lived in the same place,
But now I have two homes to call my home base.
And two cool new families where once there was one—
To be honest, I'd say I've doubled my fun.

Mom and Dad are still married, and our house is quite large,
My grandparents live here, and so does Aunt Marge.
So that's five grown-ups, two brothers, a sister and me,
Who live in this branch of our family tree.
My dad runs the kitchen, of that there's no doubt,
And we all take turns with helping him out.
Grandma's shower monitor, she makes sure we get clean;
I'm at eight, Jane's at nine, with the twins in between.
Mom and Dad are real busy, they work all the time,
We need every penny, we watch every dime.
But, we aren't poor: we've got more than we need,
"Share all that we've got," is our family creed.

Me

My cat

Chay has two parents, and Tanya has three,
I have four moms and dads who all care for me.
My dad makes my dinner, and I make my bed,
Another man lives with us, his name is Fred.
Fred's my dad's partner, they're like husband and wife,
They've been together for most of my life.
My mom visits sometimes, we all get along,
Some think we're not normal, but I think they're wrong!
We're just like the families of my friends from school,
We eat dinner together and swim in the pool.
When I'm bad I get punished and sent to my room.
On their wedding day, both my dads got to be groom!
My friends like my dads, they think that I'm lucky,
But, I think the luckiest one's my friend Chuckie!

When I was a baby, both my birth parents died,
Which means that they couldn't come back if they tried.
Their parents were too old to raise a new baby,
So these people who couldn't make kids said they'd raise me.
I started right out calling them, "Mom" and "Dad";
They're the only real parents that I've ever had.
So what if it wasn't their bodies that made me,
I know that there's nothing that would make them trade me.
'Cuz they've taught me the difference between right and wrong,
And that in this world we all want to belong
To something that's bigger than just you or me,
That we are a part of: That's our family!

I've had two mommies ever since I was born,
They mend my clothing whenever it's torn.
Donna-Mom is a lawyer, Becca-Mom likes to write,
And just like my friends and their parents we fight,
Not always, but usually over things that are small,
Like eating my green beans or can we go to the mall.
They worry about me, and sometimes they're strict,

And sometimes I don't like the clothes that they've picked.
But always there's hugging and kissing and praise
Sometimes for no reason, sometimes for good grades!
They make sure I dress warm on cold winter days,
And to tell me a story, my moms have lots of ways!
Some of my buddies have one mom and one dad,
And I've seen that they really don't have it so bad.
I wouldn't trade my family for all the whole world,
And neither would one of my bestest friends: Pearl!

My dad is my parent, the only one that I've got,
We take care of each other, I help out a lot!
He took me in when I was real small,
When nobody else cared for me at all.

He fed me and changed me and washed me by hand,
Without help from anyone, he's a single-man band!
So, I grew and I grew (as most kids that age do),
When I heard the news: that most parents are twos,
I ran home to my dad and asked, "Is it true?
Do most parents show up in boxes of two?
And if so, my dear father, what happened to you?"
Then he told me a story, I remember it well.
It was almost a good enough story to sell!

"There once was a baby, just a wee little girl,
When she was born she had been named Pearl.
Her parents were young and they lived in a place
Where people got hurt just because of their race.
So, they took their one child to save her young life,
And sent her away from that land filled with strife.

She came to America, which is where we are now,
But to find her a family, no one knew how.
Then in came this man with no kids of his own,
He was not even married, how could he give her a home?
The people in charge didn't usually give
Small children to folks who had a 'strange' way to live.
But, when they saw him hold Pearlie in his arms so strong,
They felt awful for thinking such Big Love could be wrong.
'Cuz there's Big Love and Small Love and Love-In-Between,
Big Love is so big it can clearly be seen.

"So, others may have more parents and brothers,
More daddies, and uncles, and aunts and, yes, mothers.
But none of them, no matter how it is measured,
Has ever, in all of all time, been more treasured!
And though I'm just one man, and I have just one heart,
Believe me, my miracle, you're in every part!
I hope you're not 'shamed 'cuz you've got only me?"

So, I said: "No, Daddy … I've got only *we*,
And *we* is the best thing in this world to be!
Doesn't matter if your *we* is two *she's* or one *he*!"

Art from top to bottom:

Page 29: Anna Cohen, Clarendon School, 1st Grade;
Fayzan Gowani, Clover Avenue Elementary, 5th Grade

Page 30: Nicky Solow-Collins, Ivanhoe Elementary
School, 3rd Grade; Beiji "Jimmy" Zhang, Clover
Avenue Elementary, 5th Grade; Anna Solow-Collins
(two pictures), Ivanhoe Elementary School, 1st Grade;
Siena Ko Colombier, Crossroads School, 3rd Grade

Page 31: Tia Kearns, Foundations School Community,
Kindergarten; Lazavier James, Canfield Elementary,
4th Grade; Rebeca Escala-Viñas, Clover Avenue
Elementary, 4th Grade; Margaret M. Hartley,
Crossroads School, 3rd Grade; Fanny Ballantine-
Himberg, Franklin School, 4th Grade

ODE TO PARENTS

by Billy Aronson

Sung to the tune of Beethoven's "Ode to Joy."

One or two, a mom and dad, or mom and mom, or three or two,
All that matters in a parent is they love and care for you.
Man, woman, father or mother, long as they're glad to be around,
Who cares if they make their pee-pee standing up or sitting down?

Bullfrog kids live only with their dad, who guards them as they play.
Octopus kids hang out with their mom 'til they can swim away.
Lion cubs have ten dads and moms that take turns hunting for groceries.
There are oh so many different kinds of loving families!

White or brown, it makes no diff'rence, yellow, red or ebony,
Long as they can open up a Band-Aid when you scrape your knee.
Long as they're skilled with a mop when you make a real disgusting mess,
Who cares if they wear a tie and pants or earrings and a dress?

They may walk like this, or this, or this, or this, or this, or this,
Anyway you know that they are qualified to hug and kiss.
Man, woman, father or mother, long as they're glad to be around,
Who cares if they make their pee-pee standing up or sitting down?
They love you, they're thinking of you, so you will never be alone,
There are oh so many different ways to make a loving home!

Art by James C. Ransome

GET TO KNOW ME!

Art by Sam Alper, PS#1, 5th Grade

JAMES

**I always get teased a lot
They say I'm a wussy or a girl–
It really hurts a lot.
One time when Paolo was teasing me,
Lewis stood up for me.**

LEWIS

**James is my friend,
It makes me angry when kids pick on him.
Paolo is my friend, too–
I just went up and said,
"Stop it!"**

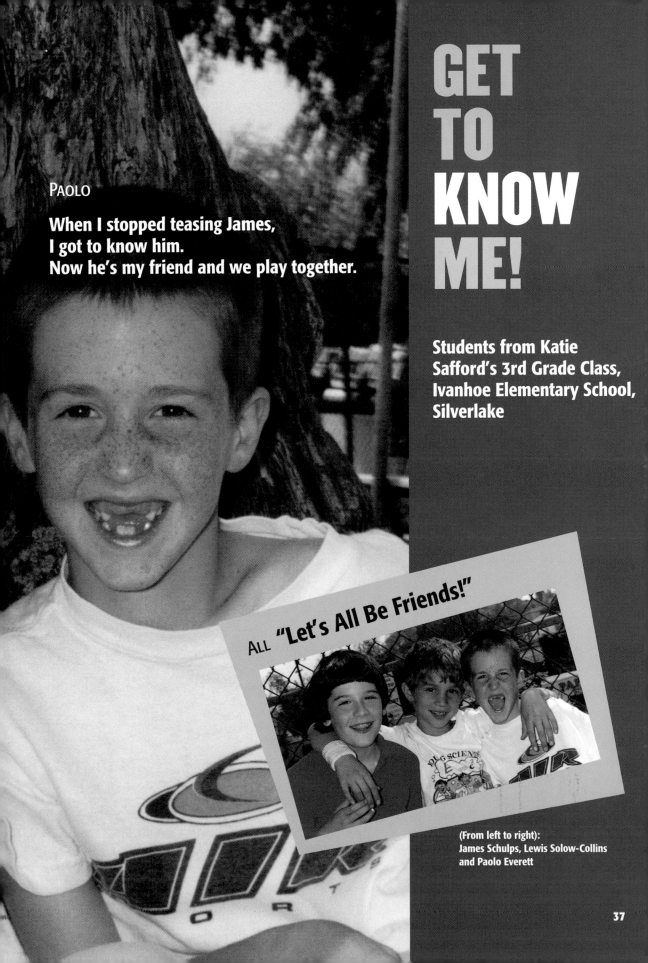

PAOLO

**When I stopped teasing James,
I got to know him.
Now he's my friend and we play together.**

GET TO KNOW ME!

**Students from Katie
Safford's 3rd Grade Class,
Ivanhoe Elementary School,
Silverlake**

ALL **"Let's All Be Friends!"**

(From left to right):
James Schulps, Lewis Solow-Collins
and Paolo Everett

37

THE GOLDEN RULE by Stacie Chaiken

Four actors (all playing the roles of children in upper elementary school) stand on the stage:

One boy wears a yarmulke *(Jewish beanie cap) and* peyes *(long sideburns). This is* JOSHUA.

One boy wears a Sikh turban to cover his long, long hair. This is NANEK.

One girl wears a beret, from under which we see long, straight blue hair, possibly in braids. She might wear a deep red lipstick. This is ANGELA.

One girl wears a smudge of ashes on her brow, vaguely suggesting a cross. She also wears a gold crucifix on a chain around her neck. This is MARY.

The actors look at the audience and at each other, pointing and making faces as if to say: "This is weird."

NANEK   See that girl with the dirt on her face? Doesn't she ever take a bath?

JOSHUA   He should talk, Diaper Head!

ANGELA   Look how his hair is all long at the sides. And that silly beanie! He looks like a nerd.

MARY   What does she think it is, Halloween?

All   They're really weird!

NANEK   *(to the audience)* They think I'm weird, but I'm not. I wear this turban—this kind of hat—because I am a Sikh. That's my religion. And if I took off my turban, you'd see I've never had a haircut, not since I was born. If I cut my hair—this is what we Sikhs believe—I will no longer be strong. *(shows his muscles)*

MARY   Wow. How long is your hair?

NANEK   *(bragging)* Down to here, I think. My sister's hair is longer, 'cuz she's older, so it's had a longer time to grow. My turban is my crown. I wear it because I am proud to be a Sikh.

MARY   How does it work? Can I try it on?

NANEK   Sure.

MARY   Now?

NANEK   Later, okay? I promise.

ANGELA   People think I'm really weird, too, because I dye my hair different colors and I like to wear hats.

NANEK   How come you do that?

ANGELA   I like the way it looks, I guess. And it's fun to keep changing how I look. I can do whatever I want and if I don't like it, I can just try something else, you know?

MARY   But why blue hair?

ANGELA   You mean instead of some "normal" color? I like doing something that says: "I'm different." I mean, we're all different in some way, right? And we should be free to be whoever we are and not have to pretend.

MARY   I know what you mean …

JOSHUA   But you said I'm weird before because of my hair and my *keepah*?

ANGELA   Is that what it's called, your beanie?

JOSHUA   Yes. Some people call it a *yarmulke*. And these are my *peyes*, my sideburns. We can never cut them. It's just like you Sikhs! I'm Jewish, but not all Jewish boys look like me. Some wear their *keepah* only when they go to synagogue, and some don't wear one at all.

MARY   Synagogue, that's like your church, right!

JOSHUA   Uh-huh.

MARY   I knew it!

JOSHUA   And some Jewish men cut their sideburns just like everyone else. But the Torah …

MARY   That's like your Bible!

NANEK   And our Guru Granth Sahib!

JOSHUA   Yeah. *(to* NANEK*)* What's a Guru Granth Sahib?

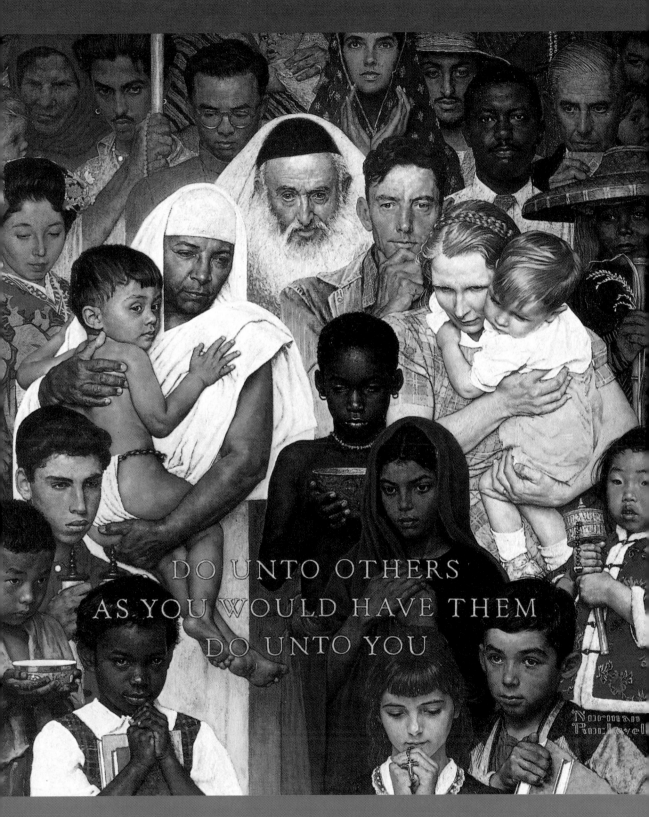

DO UNTO OTHERS
AS YOU WOULD HAVE THEM
DO UNTO YOU

NANEK   Our Sikh holy book.

JOSHUA   Okay. Like our Torah. Which says that we should never shave the corners of our beards.

ANGELA   You don't have a beard.

JOSHUA   My dad does. And I have these top corners of the beard I'll have someday, so I never cut them.

MARY   Cool, can I braid them?

JOSHUA   Yeah. That would be great! My cousin in Israel braids his!

ANGELA   If you never ever cut your hair, by the time you get old, it'll be down to your toes.

JOSHUA and NANEK   That's the idea!

ANGELA   *(to MARY)* How about you? What's that dirt on your face?

MARY   It's not dirt, it's ashes. I'm Christian, a Catholic. And I only wear ashes one day a year. On Ash Wednesday. That's the beginning of Lent, when we get ready for Easter. On Ash Wednesday, I go to church in the morning before school and the priest gives me a blessing and puts ashes on my forehead.

ANGELA   Why? Is it good for you?

MARY   Yeah, I guess so. All day, whenever I see myself in a mirror—or see someone else with ashes on—I remember to try to be a better person. That's why I wear this necklace with the cross. I wear that every day, so I can remember that I need to try really hard to treat other people well—the way I want them to treat me.

JOSHUA   Wait. We have that, too!

NANEK   So do we!

ANGELA   That's what I think, too!

JOSHUA   The Torah says: *(he sings)* "Ve'ahavta l're-akha kamokha." That's Hebrew. It means: "And you shall love your neighbor as yourself."

NANEK   That's just like the Sikhs! For us, it's karma. We say: "What you give is what you get!"

MARY   "Do unto others as you would have them do unto you."

ANGELA   That's exactly what my parents taught me. We're not religious, but ... they always say: "Don't do anything to anyone you wouldn't want them to do to you." My mom says that's the best rule to live by.

(Pause.)

JOSHUA   So I guess we don't want to be calling other people weird if we don't want to be called weird ourselves.

ANGELA, NANEK and MARY   Which we don't.

JOSHUA   Nope.

(Pause. They all nod.)

NANEK   Anyway. We're not weird. We're interesting.

(Pause. Then all in a jumble:)

ANGELA   I'm sorry I called you weird.

JOSHUA   Me, too.

MARY   Me, too.

NANEK   Me, too.

MARY   Can I see how long your hair is under that hat?

NANEK   Sure.

MARY   You think it's longer than mine? How would I look with a green stripe?

ANGELA   Could you teach me that Hebrew thing you said?

NANEK and MARY   Wait! Teach us, too! Let's all of us learn!

JOSHUA   Okay, sure: *(teaching actors and the audience the song, to a hip beat)* "Ve'ahavta"

ANGELA, NANEK, MARY and the AUDIENCE   "Ve'ahavta"

JOSHUA   "l're-akha"

ANGELA, NANEK, MARY and the AUDIENCE   "l're-akha"

JOSHUA   "kamokha"

ANGELA, NANEK, MARY and the AUDIENCE   "kamokha"

ANGELA, NANEK, MARY, JOSHUA and the AUDIENCE   *(singing)* "Ve'ahavta l're-akha kamokha."

LA PELUCA DE SU MAMA

by José Louis Ramirez

Last night, my best friend Juan came over.
And while my mom was ironing, I brushed out her wig.
When she stepped out of the room, I put her wig on
And Juan walked in.
So, I showed him: "Hey, look at this! My hair grew!"
And he just laughed.

Today, my best friend Juan made fun of me *en la escuela—*
ien frente de todos!
He told everybody: "Louis had a wig on last night—
iiiLa peluca de su mama!!!"
He told all my friends in my second-period class.
Everyone started to call me "*maricon*" and "sissy boy."
My name is Luis, and they started to call me "Luisa."
Ellos told me *que maricones* go to hell!
I sat at my desk and I put my head down and cried.

ALL THE ADAMS IN THE WORLD

Dedicated to my greatest teacher and inspiration: Adam Hillinger

Art by Kitty Suen

KID #1 and KID #2 are young teens. ADAM and INNER ADAM (ADAM's feelings that he can't express), also young teens, are dressed in the same clothes.

KID #1   Funny!

KID #2   Weird!

KID #1   Why does he do that?

INNER ADAM   Don't stare at me!

KID #1   But he's so …

KID #2   He's so …

KID #1 and KID #2 He's so …

KID #2   Funny!

KID #1   Weird!

KID #2   Why doesn't he talk?

INNER ADAM   I talk … I REALLY talk—

ADAM   *Green Eggs and Ham!*

KID #1 and KID #2 *(annoyed)* Green Eggs and Ham?

ADAM   *(building)* Casey Junior!

KID #1 and KID #2 *(taunting)* Casey Junior?

ADAM   *(angrily) The Wonderful Wizard of Oz!*

KID #1   *(directed sardonically at ADAM)* What is his problem?

(ADAM puts his index finger in his mouth and hits his head with the fist of his other hand. He is very frustrated and makes an angry, droning sound.)

KID #2   Oh … my … gosh … What … a … psycho!

(KID #1 and KID #2 give ADAM a look of total disgust and disbelief.)

INNER ADAM   *(to ADAM)* Stop it! Stop it! You're twelve years old!
                Look at the way they're looking at us! Why do you keep embarrassing us?!

ADAM   Kermit the Frog!

(Pause.)

                Tarzan!

INNER ADAM   *(shift in tone)* Precious, you're so precious. *I'm* so precious. But they can't see it.

ADAM   I want Chuckie Cheese—eight pizzas—YES!

(KID #1 and KID #2 laugh.)

INNER ADAM   Stop staring at me! Stop staring at me! Can't you see I want to fit in? I want to play and be your friend. But all I can say is:

ADAM   Jimminy Cricket!

INNER ADAM   Or …

ADAM   *The Jungle Book!*

INNER ADAM   It's all in my head and my heart—I'm just a kid who came out mis-wired!

KID #1   What a freak!

KID #2   *(whispering conspiratorially)* I hear he's artistic.

INNER ADAM	Autistic! Autistic! And it's not my fault! Please don't look at me that way!
ADAM	*(singing)* Zippidy doo dah, zippidy ay! My-oh-my what a wonderful day!
INNER ADAM	Autistic—I'm really a genius but I'm all locked up … inside of me! My language is all that I hear … memorized inside of me! But when you hear—
ADAM	*(autistic voice)* Kermit the Frog!
INNER ADAM	What I'm really saying is:
ADAM	*(in a regular, warm and compassionate voice)* "It's not easy being green!"
INNER ADAM	It's so hard to be different, to not fit in, to be like a frog, judged by your appearance. And when you hear—
ADAM	*(autistic voice) The Jungle Book!*
INNER ADAM	What I'm telling you is to:
ADAM	*(in fun and vivacious singing voice)* Look for the bare necessities, The simple bare necessities! Forget about your worries and your strife!
INNER ADAM	And even when you hear—
ADAM	*(autistic voice)* TARZAN!
INNER ADAM	I'm telling you that: "You'll be in my heart—"
ADAM	*(singing)* "Yes, you'll be in my heart—"
INNER ADAM	Don't you get it? I'm reaching out to you—trying to connect—in the only way I know how. But it all makes sense to me.
KID #1	What's "autistic"?
KID #2	My mom says he's in a world of his own. She doesn't know how his parents can love him. She thinks they should put him in an institution and get on with their lives.
KID #1	Funny!
KID #2	Weird!
KID #1	Why does he do that?
INNER ADAM	If only they could listen!
KID #1	But he's so …
KID #2	He's so …
KID #1 and KID #2	He's so …

(KID #1 and KID #2 exit together.)

ADAM	*(singing)* When you wish upon a star Makes no difference who you are When you wish upon a star Your dreams come true …
INNER ADAM	*(lovingly puts arm around ADAM)* Jimminy Cricket!

DOING THE RIGHT THING

by Cynthia Ruffin and the Gutierrez Family, based on a true story and developed through improvisation with Fringe Benefits

Three or more young Bullies circle the stage, pointing at each other, the audience members, imaginary children and/or at ANTONIA. ANTONIA (TONIA), a fifth grade girl, stands center. ALFONSO, her brother, is in ninth grade.

BULLY #1 Geek!

BULLY #2 Sissy!

BULLY #3 Shamu!

BULLY #1 Toothpick!

BULLY #2 Stupid!

BULLY #3 Loser!

BULLY #1 *¡Chino!*

BULLY #2 Towel-head!

BULLY #3 Nerd!

BULLY #1 Fairy!

BULLY #2 Girl!

BULLY #3 4-Eyes!

BULLY #1 Redneck!

BULLY #2 Dog!

BULLY #3 *¡Gorda!*

BULLY #1 *¡Flaco!*

BULLY #2 Lezbo!

BULLY #3 *¡Mariposa!*

BULLY #1 Retard!

BULLY #2 Queer boy!

BULLY #3 Nappy Head!

BULLY #1 Wetback!

ALL BULLIES FAGGOT!

(The BULLIES exit, leaving ANTONIA alone on stage.)

TONIA   *(to audience)* Have you ever been called a name that wasn't very nice? Something really awful and mean? I have. It's not even anything about me, really, but it still hurts real bad. I mean, it doesn't even have anything to do with me. Well, it kinda does. *(pause)* My name's Antonia and my brother, Alfonso, is gay.

(ALFONSO enters.)

Being gay means that he likes other guys. Y'know, like to be their boyfriend and to hold their hand and stuff. When I was younger I remember wondering how he turned that way. So I asked him one day … *(to ALFONSO)* Alfonso, what happened to you to make you turn gay?

ALFONSO   *(a little angry)* Nothing happened to make me *turn* gay! *(softening)* Sorry, Tonia, I didn't mean to snap at you, but so many people ask that question. Nothing happened to make me *turn* gay, I've always been gay … Since the day I was born, I think. I've always liked guys. It's always felt right. Y'know? *(he exits)*

TONIA   *(to audience)* My brother's always been gay. And I've always been his little sister. And that brings us to the name-calling. You see, Alfonso used to go to Saint Ignatius School, too, and everyone knew that he was gay. And why shouldn't they? *They* don't have to hide anything about themselves when they come to school, why should he have to hide who he is? Well, they used to call him awful names and now they call *me* awful names. Sometimes other kids, too. I don't get into fights or anything like that, but I sure don't let them get away with calling me or my brother names.

(A GIRL BULLY and a BOY BULLY enter.)

GIRL   Eeeeeewww! Look who's here!! It's Lezzie!!

BOY   Be careful, she might kiss you! Ha ha!

TONIA   I'm not a lesbian!

GIRL   Yes you are! Your brother's a fag, so that makes you one, too!

TONIA   My brother is gay.

BOY   That's what she said: *(doing a limp-wristed, lisping parody)* "He's GAY!"

TONIA   What's your problem? Why are you so mean?

GIRL   We're not the ones with the problem.

BOY   Don't show her your legs, she'll fall in love with you!

GIRL   Eeewww! Gross!

TONIA   Not even my dog would fall in love with you!

GIRL   *(in TONIA's face, serious fighting energy)* You take that back!

TONIA   You take back what you said!

BOY   Fight! Fight!

(Their teacher, MR. KENT, comes over to intervene when he hears the fighting.)

TEACHER   What's going on here?

TONIA   Mr. Kent, they're calling me names!

TEACHER   Andy, Carla, you know you're not supposed to be calling people names.

BOY and GIRL   We didn't do anything!

TONIA   Yes you did! You called me a lezzie!

TEACHER   *(to BULLIES, nervous, unsure of how to handle this)* Uh … uh … Why did you say that?

TONIA   Just because my brother is gay.

TEACHER   Uh … uh …

(School bell rings.)

Time to go back to class … Recess is over.

(BULLIES whisper, "Lezzie" and "Dyke" to TONIA behind the TEACHER's back.)

TONIA   They're doing it again! Make them stop!

TEACHER   C'mon, c'mon … back to class, kids … *(ushers the BULLIES offstage to class)*

TONIA   When the kids were making fun of Scott 'cuz he wears glasses, you made *them* stop!

(TONIA steps downstage and talks to the audience again. The BULLIES laugh as they exit.)

That happens to me every day! Sometimes I get so mad, I just want to scream at all of

them, "What's the matter with you?! Are you afraid someone's gonna think *you're* gay if you're friends with the girl who has a gay brother?!" Sometimes I get mad at myself. I feel like I should make them stop and make them understand that my brother is a lot of fun and that they would probably really like him. And sometimes I get mad at Alfonso. I start thinking that if he were just normal– *(catches herself, pause)* And then, I remember that he is normal. Perfectly normal.

MOTHER   *(calling to her from offstage)* Tonia!

(MOTHER and FATHER enter. MOTHER is very jovial and good natured, the kind of mom everyone wishes she had. FATHER is large in build, gregarious and warm. He has a wonderful spirit that fills the room.)

Tonia! There you are, *m'hija*! Didn't you hear me calling you? How was your day today?

TONIA   *(running to her mother, near tears)* Oh, Mommy!

MOTHER   *¿Qué pasa,* sweetie? What's wrong?

TONIA   They were calling me names again!

FATHER   Did you tell anyone?

TONIA   Yeah, I told my teacher, Mr. Kent.

FATHER   What did he do?

TONIA   Nothing. Again! I'm so sick of this!

Art by Gabrielle Veit-Bermúdez

MOTHER	I know. It must be really hard for you. I can't even imagine how hard.
TONIA	They never stop!
MOTHER	They're so mean. And you're so brave. You're the bravest little girl I know!
TONIA	I'm tired of being brave. I wanna go to a different school, like Alfonso did!
FATHER	Don't you think that would be like running away?
TONIA	Yes, but I don't care.
FATHER	You know, I've had just about enough of this. It's ridiculous for our daughter to go to school and not feel safe there.
MOTHER	How can anyone learn in a place where bullies run the school and the teachers don't help you?!
FATHER	Lydia, I think we have to do something about this. This is not what we taught our children. We taught them that people should be recognized for their acts of kindness and their tolerance, not discriminated against for being different. Their school *says* they "celebrate diversity," but now this same school, this very good school, is *showing* them something completely different. *(sighs heavily)*
MOTHER	Are you thinking what I'm thinking?

(FATHER nods agreement; MOTHER and FATHER move into a new tableau with MR. KENT.)

TONIA	*(to audience)* So my mom and dad went to my school the very next day. My parents were great. They told my teacher:

FATHER	*(to TEACHER)* Everybody deserves respect, no matter who you are, what your job is, what color your skin is, or if you're straight or gay.
MOTHER	*(to TEACHER)* And everybody has to respect you … Not just the other children, but even the teachers and the principal and the janitors. Everybody.
TONIA	And something in what my parents said made Mr. Kent change his mind, I think–

(PARENTS and MR. KENT shake hands.)

TONIA	'Cuz now when the other kids start teasing me, he tells them that they have to stop.
TEACHER	Andy!!!

(The TEACHER strides offstage to deal with ANDY.)

TONIA	The other day, he even made that bully Andy apologize to me.

(ALFONSO reenters and joins family.)

	Right now, I'm working on an oral report about Ellen DeGeneres, Elton John, Melissa Etheridge and other famous gay and lesbian people. I'm doing the report because of my brother, but I'm also doing it because kids need to understand that people who are gay are normal, and so are their families. When I told my mom what my oral report was about, she said:
MOTHER	Are you sure you want to do this?
TONIA	Of course. I'm proud of my brother. And if this can help another kid, it's important to do it.

The Gutierrez Family (left to right):
Natalie, Mom Lydia, Dad Mike, and Julian

COOTIES

Excerpted from *Cooties* by John Fleck

MAMA enters on her knees scrubbing the floor with a sponge. She scrubs her way across the stage. She wears rubber kitchen gloves.

Author's Note: I would cast a man in the role of MAMA, but that interpretation is entirely up to you.

MAMA   Cooties, cooties everywhere:
They're on your skin, they're in his hair!

Cooties, cooties, crawlin' 'round!
They got six legs, and a big ugly frown!

They're hairy, they're scary, they'll rip you to shreds!
They lurk in the dark right under your beds!

(As she squeezes out her dirty sponge, she talks to the audience as if she's a preacher's wife, instructing a little child in the ways of the dirty world.)

Cooties. Dirty, dirty, cooties!

Art by Mark Tapio Kines

You get cooties from people who are different from you—weird, icky, *different* people.

You can get cooties by touching someone who has cooties … or by coming in contact with an object that may have been touched by a person who has cooties, like a school book or a dirty floor upon which they might walk!

It's always good to carry a good portable can of disinfectant *(spraying Lysol)* it helps!

Never, never share a meal with someone who has cooties. Never use the same silverware or dishes.

Oh, and it's good to wear gloves—I prefer plastic—if you have to go to a person's house who has cooties. Never touch a doorknob with bare skin. *(sprays Lysol again and then goes back to scrubbing)*

Cooties are highly contagious!

Never, never, never stand too close to someone who has cooties. Wear a mask!

'Cuz, once you get cooties, you can't get rid of them! You might as well wear a big ol' "C" on your head, a big sparkly scarlet "C" on a hairband!: "C" for *cooties*! dirty … dirty cooties …

(MAMA exits, scrubbing furiously, muttering, "Dirty, dirty cooties … "

GIRL or BOY enter and speak to the audience:)

GIRL or BOY   This just in:

You can't get cooties by touching someone who's *different* from you, or by breathing in their air! That's just a silly, old superstition!

Cooties are just bed bugs.

You don't get cooties 'cuz you hang out with kids who are different from you! Just 'cuz a kid looks really different from you, or wears funny-looking clothes, or comes from another country, or believes in a different religion than you, or if she only has one leg, or if he likes to skip rope instead of play football—doesn't mean he or she is gonna give you COOTIES!!

Cooties are just bed bugs. You get 'em if you don't wash your sheets often enough!

This has been a public service announcement from "Mothers Against Dirty Laundry." Thank you.

Oh, yeah … Don't forget to make your bed!

THE BIRTHDAY PARTY

Story by Jamice Lamara Jefferson with stage adaptation by Mark E. Rosenthal

JAMICE My name is Jamice. This is the story of my birthday party that just happened last week. It was a slumber party. My mom said I could invite six people over on Friday night and they could stay till Saturday night. Six people isn't a lot. So, I had to choose carefully. It wasn't hard to decide, though. I decided to ask Tiffany and Nicole, my two best friends from school, and Robyn, Kai, Rachel and Lupe, 'cuz I've known them forever. We've all lived in the same neighborhood since we were in kindergarten, but we go to different schools now. They had never met Tiffany or Nicole. So, two weeks before the party, I spent all day cutting and pasting and coloring. My invitations were beautiful. Before I sent them off, I showed them to my mother and my aunt.

MOM These are beautiful, Jamice. Are you sure you want to send them in the mail? They might get ruined.

AUNT Mary, don't beat around the bush. If you have something to say to the child, say it. *(MOM just glares at AUNT)* Fine. Jamice, honey, you know those girls won't come to your party.

JAMICE Which girls?

AUNT The ones from your new school … Tiffany and Nicole.

JAMICE Of course they will. They're my best friends.

MOM Jamice, I think your aunt is right. Best friends or not, they won't come to Compton.

JAMICE You don't even know them. How can you say they won't come?

MOM *(delicately)* Lots of times, people who don't live here … are afraid to visit people who do.

JAMICE Why?

AUNT 'Cuz the only things they ever hear about this neighborhood are bad things. So, they don't think it's safe.

JAMICE But, I've lived here my whole life and nothing bad's ever happened to me. *(MOM and AUNT look away)* I think you're wrong. They'll come to my party. You'll see.

(to audience) All next week at school I waited for Tiffany and Nicole to get their invitations. Robyn, Kai, Rachel and Lupe had already received theirs and said they'd be there. I couldn't wait for my old friends to meet my new ones. I knew they'd get along. But, I was beginning to think my invitations had been lost in the mail. It was the week of my party and Nicole and Tiffany still hadn't received theirs. Then, on the Monday before the party, I heard the news. *(rushing in, breathless)* Mom! Mom, did anyone call while I was at school?

MOM *(stops what she is doing)* Yes, Jamice. They called. Finally.

JAMICE See! I told you they would! I knew you were wrong about them.

AUNT Jamice, we weren't the ones who were wrong.

(JAMICE understands.)

(gently) Honey, we told you not to get your hopes up.

MOM *(putting her arm around her daughter)* We've lived here a lot longer than you, Jamice. We do know a few things about the way the world works.

JAMICE   (close to tears) Did they say why?

(AUNT and MOM exchange a look.)

MOM   Tiffany has a wedding to go to and Nicole … well, her mother can't drive her this far.

JAMICE   Oh …

(Pause. Then to audience:)

I didn't talk to Tiffany or Nicole for the rest of that week. I couldn't even look at them. I had gone to both of their parties and neither one of them was coming to mine. When I was leaving school on Friday, I saw them. They looked like they had something to say to me … something like, "Sorry." But, they didn't come up to me and I was way too angry to be the only one doing the traveling *again*. So, we just looked at each other and went our separate ways. But, I didn't let them ruin my party. That night, Robyn, Kai, Rachel, Lupe and I gave each other green clay facials, and drank sparkling apple cider and played Jenga and Twister and had a really great time. But, I couldn't help thinking that any minute Tiffany and Nicole were gonna knock on the door and say: "SURPRISE!" And, I'd feel bad for having doubted them. Well, I didn't have to worry about that 'cuz they never did show up. The next Monday, at lunch, I saw Tiffany and Nicole eating together and laughing. As soon as they saw me, though, they stopped. Like I had caught them doing something wrong.

(to the girls) I wish you could've come to my party. I missed you and we had a lot of fun.

TIFFANY   (ashamed) Sorry …

NICOLE   (also ashamed) Yeah. Sorry, Jamice. We both *really* wanted to come—

TIFFANY   But, our parents wouldn't let us.

NICOLE   I wanted to say something to you last week. But, I just couldn't.

TIFFANY   I couldn't, either. Every time I saw you I just wanted to hide.

JAMICE   Why? Why couldn't you come?

TIFFANY   My mom said it was too dangerous.

NICOLE   My parents said that people with skin this color (indicates her own) aren't safe in Compton.

JAMICE   Well, I went to your neighborhoods! Do you think those are friendly places for people with skin this color? (indicates her own) Tiffany, did you know a policeman followed my mother's car all the way to your front door and didn't leave until I had gone inside? And, Nicole, your neighbors were looking at me like they thought I was gonna rob them. But, I didn't *care*! I wasn't visiting to make *them* happy. I was there for my friends. And, it's not fair … that my friends couldn't be there for me.

TIFFANY   (almost crying) Oh, gosh, Jamice … I'm sorry!

NICOLE   I'm sorry, too! I swear I am so sorry!

TIFFANY   Will you give us another chance?

JAMICE   I only have one birthday.

NICOLE   I know … but, Tiffany and I have a plan. If you'll invite us over again, I SWEAR …

TIFFANY   Me, too, I SWEAR …

NICOLE   I'll convince my parents to let me spend the night at your place.

TIFFANY   Me, too.

NICOLE   I know we've let you down.

TIFFANY   But, give us another chance. We'll make it up to you.

NICOLE   I don't want to lose you as a friend, just 'cuz of what my parents are afraid of.

JAMICE   (to the audience) So, the next weekend Tiffany and her mom, and Nicole and her mom and dad all came over to my house for dinner. It was really neat, too. After dinner, Nicole and Tiffany's folks let them sleep over and we all went to lunch the next day, too. I guess when they explained to their parents how much that party meant to me, and how hurt I was that they didn't come, they understood. See! … I WAS RIGHT ABOUT MY FRIENDS AFTER ALL!

THE WAR OF THE STUCK-UP NOSES

by Mark Imme with Mark E. Rosenthal

NARRATOR   It was the worst of times, it was the best of times at Bel Air Prep. What this school needed was a change. And that's exactly what they got.

SCENE ONE
Bel Air Prep: A Classroom

MR. HALL   Class, today is the second day of the second month. You know what that means …

(The students stare at him in silence. We hear crickets.)

MR. HALL   Okay. Who's going to go first?

COCO   I will, like always.

MR. HALL   Okay. Good. *(Coco leaps up)* Coco, why don't you go first? I'll just … sit over here.

COCO   So. Today for show-and-tell I will tell you about what my parents do and show you their fabulous coins.

(Students sigh.)

This is the first nickel my father ever earned. It's solid gold … My father is so rich. My mother is, too. My dad is a plastic surgeon, and my mother runs the Chanel Modeling Agency. Enough said! And I only wear the very *best* jeans—you can tell by the dollar sign on the back pocket—

(The door opens and NANCY CAMPBELL enters the room. Her clothes are mismatched—patterns clash with stripes over a battleground of bright colors. Her hair is short. She wears glasses and no makeup. She walks with her eyes cast downward. When she turns around, we see a large "L" on the back pocket of her jeans.)

MR. HALL   *(cuts in)* Oh, yes! Our new student is here. Everyone meet Nancy Campbell.

COCO   *Excuse me*, Mr. Hall!

MR. HALL   Yes, Coco?

COCO   I was talking—

MR. HALL   I noticed that, but—

COCO   *(looking offstage)* Mr. Hall! There's a moose running towards the principal's office!

MR. HALL   Don't PANIC!!! I'll be right back. *(exits)*

NANCY   Gee, I'm sorry. I didn't mean to interrupt.

COCO   The damage is already done. *(to NANCY)* Does that "L" on your butt stand for "Loser" or "Lame"? *(students laugh; NANCY is ashamed)* She is giving us *ghetto*! Did your mother go shopping by braille?

GIRL   *(chimes in)* Nice outfit! Who shot the couch?

BOY   Did that shirt come with your Happy Meal?

COCO   Wait, you guys. This one's the best. *(dramatic pause)* Looks like somebody's found the softer side of Sears!

(Students laugh; NANCY withers. Bell rings and class is over.)

SCENE TWO
On the Playground

COCO (entering) Hi, Brittany. Hi, Victoria. How are my two best friends doing?

BRITTANY Fine.

VICTORIA Fine, I guess.

COCO What do you mean, "you guess"?

VICTORIA Well, Coco, you really should have been nicer to that new girl.

COCO What new girl?

VICTORIA That Nancy-what's-her-name.

COCO Oh, that Nancy Nothing. (laughs) That's what she is—nothing!

BRITTANY (admiringly) Gee, Coco, you're so mean!

COCO (flattered) I know, huh!?

VICTORIA Well, anyways, I kind of like her. I mean she seems nice and all.

COCO Nice? Nice!? Next thing you know, you'll be hanging out with her and wearing matching Kmart outfits. Nice doesn't win any awards. I am not nice and I don't want to have friends who are! I am *popular*! You don't become popular by being *nice*! And I didn't work this hard to become popular to have *you* blow it for me by hanging out with trash like that.

VICTORIA I don't get it.

COCO Victoria, darling, if you even dare to look at Ms. Nancy Nothing, I will make sure all of Bel Air Prep knows you are a traitor and a reject!

VICTORIA What!?

COCO Don't test me, sweetie.

VICTORIA Whatever.

COCO And Brittany, that rule goes for you, too! I'm warning you, both! You want to bask in my sunshine, then you've gotta play by my rules—or you'll get burned.

BRITTANY Gosh, Victoria. You can never keep your mouth shut, can you?

VICTORIA Brittany!?

(NANCY enters.)

NANCY Hi, Victoria.

(VICTORIA stiffens.)

(louder and more cheery) Hi, Victoria!

COCO She heard you!

NANCY Oh.

BRITTANY Gee, what's that horrible smell? Oh, of course, it must be Nancy's smellacious clothes! *(laughs)*

COCO Good one, Brittany. You have pleased me. You get a lipstick! *(hands it to her)*

VICTORIA You guys. That wasn't funny.

COCO *(loudly and in disbelief)* Excuse me, Victoria. What did you say? I can barely HEAR you over that girl's outfit. It's so LOUD!

(Coco and BRITTANY laugh.)

VICTORIA *(sadly)* I said, "How funny!"

COCO That's what I thought you said! *(gives VICTORIA the evil eye)* No lipstick for you. If you'd kept your mouth shut, you wouldn't have worn it all away.

NANCY So, where are you guys going?

COCO Wherever you're not, sweetie!

BRITTANY Ummm, *hello*! NEWS FLASH! Nancy, we don't like you, so don't talk to or follow us.

NANCY Why not? What did I ever do to you?

COCO Honey, it's what you won't do to us. You wouldn't ask the Queen of England to hang around with Oscar the Grouch, would you? Go back to your trash can.

BRITTANY Yeah, you look like a boy. Are you sure you're not a boy?

COCO Let's go, you two. If we stick around here much longer, people are going to think we're with her, and the janitor will take *us all* to the garbage dump. —To the shopping mall!

(Coco and BRITTANY exit.)

VICTORIA 'Bye, Nancy. *(starts to walk away)*

NANCY *(pulls VICTORIA's arm gently)* Why do you always do what Coco says?!

VICTORIA	I'm sorry. But, she told me if I talk to you, my reputation here will be destroyed. She'll do it, too!
NANCY	My mother always used to tell me, "Never let another mind make yours up!" Do you understand?
VICTORIA	Look, I'd better go … umm … 'Bye!

(NANCY, now alone on stage, writes in her diary.)

NANCY	Dear Diary, I miss my old school. My friends weren't rich … but they liked me. *(sobs)*
VICTORIA	*(sneaks back in and crosses to NANCY)* Hey … don't cry.
NANCY	Everyone hates me.
VICTORIA	I don't hate you, Nancy. It's just that …
NANCY	Just what? Just my hair? Just my clothes? No, let me guess … Just *me*! Well, I can't change who I am!
VICTORIA	Look, I used to be just like you. But, ever since Coco took me under her wing, I've been popular, and I've gone to parties and had friends …
NANCY	And, you're afraid to lose all of that … just for being nice to me. I understand.
VICTORIA	*(sadly)* I guess you do.

(Pause.)

	I've just decided something. I don't care what anybody else says. I like you, Nancy Campbell, and I'd be honored to have you as a friend.
NANCY	Really?
VICTORIA	Really and truly. And if Coco doesn't like it … she can lump it. Friends, right? *(extends her hand)*
NANCY	Friends! *(shakes VICTORIA's hand)*

(Bell rings.)

SCENE THREE
Back to the Classroom

Noisy students rush on stage, past NANCY and VICTORIA, creating a "classroom" around them. Some kids stand between them and the "door."

MR. HALL	Okay, class! Settle down!
COCO	Victoria! *(storms through the group, roughly pushing people aside)* Mr. Hall … Principal Hassenflass wants to see you in her office.
MR. HALL	Oh! I'd better go, then. I'll be right back. You kids stay out of trouble while I'm gone. *(exits)*
CLASS	We will, Mr. Hall! *(when the coast is clear)* FIGHT! FIGHT!
COCO	Whoa! Hold on! I'll tell you when there's gonna be a fight. Victoria … is it true?
VICTORIA	Is what true?
COCO	YOU KNOW PERFECTLY WELL WHAT! Did you break my rule and talk to "it"?
VICTORIA	I don't know anyone named "it."
COCO	DID YOU TALK TO NANCY NOTHING RIGHT UNDER MY NOSE WHILE MY BACK WAS TURNED?
VICTORIA	*(proudly)* Yes, so what!?
COCO	SO WHAT?!!! YOU ARE OUT! OUT OF THE GROUP! OFF OF THE TEAM! YOU WILL NEVER AGAIN GO TO THE MALL WITH US, OR HAVE SLEEPOVERS AT MY HOUSE, OR USE MY NAIL POLISH!
VICTORIA	FINE! BECAUSE NOW I HAVE SOMETHING THAT'S BETTER THAN ALL OF THOSE THINGS!!!!
COCO	AS IF! *(to the rest of the class)* I need a replacement friend. Who wants to take Vicky's place in *my* group? *(girls clamor)*
VICTORIA	I have a real friend. Her name is Nancy. And she's worth more than fifty Cocos.
NANCY	Thanks, Victoria.
VICTORIA	No problem, Nancy. *(to class)* Oh, and one more thing, guys—"Coco's" real name is *Agnes*! She's been lying to us all for years!

(Coco gasps, horrified.)

BOY   *Agnes?!* I wonder what else she lied about?

GIRL   Yeah! *(murmurs of agreement)* Your name is fake and so are you!

(Voices from the crowd: "Liar!" "Forget her!" "I knew she was fake all along!" Coco is left alone with BRITTANY. NANCY and VICTORIA stand apart from them.)

BRITTANY   Why would you lie about your name?

COCO   Because AGNES is an ugly girl name, and I am NOT UGLY!!

BRITTANY   My mom's name is Agnes, and she's beautiful.

(NANCY and VICTORIA cross over to COCO.)

NANCY   *(gently)* You know what, Coco—I mean *Agnes*? I'm proud of who I am. You can't ever take that away from me. Maybe, you should try liking yourself. 'Cuz, if you keep acting the way you've been acting, pretty soon no one else will have anything to do with you.

(VICTORIA moves NANCY away from COCO.)

VICTORIA   I'm proud of you, Nancy! You sure told her! Let's go to my place. We can make chocolate chip cookies to celebrate!

NANCY   Okay! I'd like that!

BRITTANY   Umm … Can I go, too?

VICTORIA   Nancy, is it okay with you if Brittany comes with us?

NANCY   Well, sure, but … that's not up to me to decide.

BRITTANY   I'm sorry I was so mean to you.

NANCY   You won't make fun of me, will you?

BRITTANY   I promise I won't. Promise you won't treat me like a flunkie and boss me around like Coco?!

NANCY   I promise! In our new group, we'll all be equal.

BRITTANY   And we won't make fun of anybody.

VICTORIA   And our group will be open to everybody, as long as they're nice!

COCO   Hey, Brittany … what about me?

BRITTANY   *(weary, but not mean)* What about you?

COCO   You need me! You're nothing without me! Do you hear me?! Nothing, I said!!!

BRITTANY   If we are nothing without you—

VICTORIA, BRITTANY and NANCY   —then that's good enough for us!!!

(The three laugh and walk away arm-in-arm. Coco is left by herself in disbelief.)

FAIR PLAY

an interactive exercise for 3rd to 6th grade students

by Norma Bowles with input from Dana Gallagher, developed through improvisation with Fringe Benefits and *Cootie Shots* company members

The front yard of a house in a neighborhood with lots of kids. A fourth grade BOY and GIRL run on stage playing with a couple of dolls. They should be having such a good time that anybody watching them would want to jump in.

BOY   *(evil character voice)* I'm gonna catch you, and when I do … I'm gonna make you clean all of Gotham City with a toothbrush!

GIRL   Oh, no you're not! I'm surrounding you with the Web of Goodness! *(makes her doll run around his fifteen or twenty times)*

BOY   Aaaargh! You've got me in your Web … I'm becoming a good guy!

GIRL   When you're ready to be good, *you* can clean all of Gotham City! And, I'll even let you use a mop. 'Cuz I'm Super Fair Super Girl!

Art by Chris Müller

BOY	Okay. I'm good now. Let me out. *(she does)* Now, you get captured by the evil Dr. Plomulak, and I'll save you.
GIRL	You saved me last time. Now, it's my turn to save you.
BOY	How about if we both save someone together?!
GIRL	Okay! Let's save Gordon!
BOY	Why would Dr. Plomulak kidnap a cat?
GIRL	'Cuz Gordon has special powers!
BOY	Like what?
GIRL	*(with a sense of mystery)* He can see the future. He has an early warning system. He always knows when something bad's gonna happen. *(they see the cat flee the stage)* Hey, Gordon! Come back here!
BOY	*(seeing the BULLY enter)* Uh-oh. I think his early warning wasn't early enough.

(BULLY enters with his FRIEND. BOY and GIRL continue to play, but we can no longer hear their dialogue. At some point, BULLY grabs the doll from the BOY and plays Keep-Away. He says mean things to impress his FRIEND. FRIEND, BOY and GIRL are tongue-tied.)

BULLY	*(to FRIEND)* Look at the little girls playing dollies! Watch this! *(grabs BOY's doll, BOY reaches for it)* Want it? *(BOY almost gets it, but BULLY yanks it back)* Psych! *(to BOY)* Only girls play with dollies! Are you a little girl, Gabriel?! Gaaaaaaayyyyy-briel! Gaylord Gabriel!!!! Do you know what happens to little sissy boys who play with dolls? They grow up to wear dresses … and nobody likes them! Why aren't you playing with the guys? Won't they let you? She's just playing with you 'cuz she feels sorry for you. Ooooh, the little baby's gonna cry now! Come on … cry for us, sissy!
FRIEND	*(to BULLY, BOY and GIRL)* FREEZE!

(BULLY, BOY and GIRL freeze.)

(to audience) I don't know why my friend picks on Gabriel. It's so stupid and it makes *everyone* feel crummy! I wish I knew what to say to stop him! Do you have any suggestions about what I could say or do that would make him stop being a bully? I mean, I don't want to lose his friendship or anything, but I hate it when he does this! Raise your hand if you have an idea!

(FRIEND solicits suggestions from the audience and gets people up on stage to take his/her place and see how they could implement their strategies. BULLY, BOY and GIRL, react in character to the new strategies. They don't capitulate too quickly, but if a reasonable "intervention" is attempted, the actors show how the scene could end more happily, if possible with everyone being friends. If someone suggests a less positive intervention [return BULLY's name-calling, a move to violence, etc.], the negative impact on everyone should also be shown.

Note: FRIEND needs to caution the audience that no real violence, personal put-downs or swear words may be used. Violent interventions should be done only by the cast, not with volunteers from the audience.

Following are some of the interventions FRIEND should get the volunteers to try:

1. violence;
2. name-calling;
3. bringing in an adult;
4. taking BULLY away to do something else;
5. standing up for BOY;
6. joining the game and encouraging BULLY to join the game, too;
7. telling BULLY that what he's doing isn't funny or cool;
8. standing up for BOY and GIRL, saying it's okay to play whatever one likes to play;
9. helping BULLY understand how he would feel if he were being picked on.)

CAP'N CRUNCH

A POEM BY BONNIE EATON

Excerpted from *Appearances* by Paula Weston Solano

Bonnie's voice-over is heard while she silently eats cereal and watches TV.

After school, aftermath, after everyone's gone,
It's always the same: get home, throw down my coat, turn on TV,
Get out the bowl, get out the milk, the Cap'n Crunch,
Get on the floor, the coffee table, the television
It's too quiet in here, so I turn it up loud.
I'm not like the Brady girls—Marcia, Jan, Cindy-blond or even Ginger-red
But Mary Ann—dark, Mary Ann, I guess I'm like Mary Ann ... on the island.
Dumb TV—
It laughs at me, "No one's here, no one's coming,"
'Til late, 'til you're asleep, 'til you can't see or speak, or ...
I hate going to sleep without a kiss and I hate school,
I hate the boys who call me, "Fatty, fatty, two-by-four."
And I hate this time between.
Recess sucks and I hate kickball and dodge ball
And anything where people get picked.
No one's home, it echoes here:
Chicken potpie tins piled in the sink,
Socks lying on the floor.
I don't feel fat.
It's so empty in the living room that used to be the dining room—
When Daddy's chair was next to Mom's and mine,
At the table where Daddy took Polaroids of me
Unwrapping my new Barbie house, while Mom cut the cake
And everyone sang, before we all got moved around.
Only I still dine here.
Is it dining when you do it all the time?
Or just when you do it with others?
Or just at certain times?
Cereal goes on forever, like the reruns on TV.

(BONNIE continues eating and staring blankly at the television as lights fade to black.)

ANYONE FOR DOUBLE DUTCH?

by Carl Andress

A school yard playground at recess. We hear the sounds of elementary school children at play. MIKE, a fourth grader, stands alone tossing a football into the air. He is waiting for someone to play with. After a moment, PAUL enters. He is a bookish third grader, his face buried in a paperback book: A Cricket in Times Square*. He also carries a Thermos and has a book bag slung over his shoulder. MIKE eyes PAUL as he sits on the ground and pours Kool-Aid from his Thermos into its accompanying cup, never taking his eyes off the book. MIKE considers approaching PAUL but waits to see if anybody else will show up. He finally gives up.*

Note: In the original production, the jump ropes for double Dutch were mimed.

MIKE   Hey. Go long.

PAUL   I'm sorry?

MIKE   I said, "Go long."

PAUL   Are you speaking to me?

MIKE   Yeah, I said, "Go long."

PAUL   Is that supposed to mean something?

MIKE   You never heard about going long?

PAUL   No, I haven't.

MIKE   Don't you play football?

PAUL   No.

MIKE   You don't?!

PAUL   Sorry to disappoint you.

MIKE   All boys play football. Is there something wrong with you?

PAUL   Not that I'm aware of.

MIKE   Just catch the ball.

PAUL   All right. I'll try. *(puts his book down)*

MIKE   Cool. *(gets into position to throw the ball to PAUL)*

PAUL   There's only one problem—

MIKE   Heads up!

(MIKE throws the ball to PAUL. The ball hits PAUL in the head and knocks him down.)

PAUL   I don't catch so good. Oww!

MIKE   C'mon! Get up! Throw me the ball, throw me the ball!

PAUL   *(grabbing the ball)* Okay, you asked for it.

(PAUL tosses the ball to MIKE. The ball lands at MIKE's feet. He picks it up.)

MIKE   You call that a throw? C'mon, go long!

PAUL   What does that mean?

MIKE   *(gives up trying to explain)* Just stand there.

(Instead of trying to explain, MIKE shakes his head and moves to catch a pass. NICOLE and ANN, two fourth graders, enter. They hold hands and giggle. ANN carries a jump rope.)

NICOLE   Hey! Let's jump rope. Over here.

ANN   Who'll we play with? Oh, there's Paul.

NICOLE   Hey, Paul!

(PAUL, by some fluke, has managed to catch the ball. He is beaming. When he hears NICOLE say, "Hey, PAUL!" he looks over to see her … just in time to get surprise-tackled by MIKE.)

PAUL   (from ground) Oooo, Ow! Will you please stop bumping into me?!

MIKE   This is how you play football! I'm trying to teach you the game.

ANN   What are you guys doing?

MIKE   What does it look like?

PAUL   I'm taking a time-out!

MIKE   Come on, get up. Don't be a wuss! You gotta be tough! You gotta be a man!

ANN   Come with us, Paul. We need a third for jump rope. You in?

PAUL   You bet!

MIKE   What? You just dropping me? I haven't shown you how to score a touchdown yet.

(MIKE demonstrates a strut.)

PAUL   If it's got anything to do with falling down, then I'm already an expert.

MIKE   Hey, don't go! Hang with me.

ANN   You can play with us if you want.

MIKE   No thanks.

NICOLE   Suit yourself.

MIKE   Wait a minute. (to PAUL) You're gonna jump rope?

PAUL   Sure.

MIKE   With them?

NICOLE   Something wrong with jumping rope?

PAUL   You need another rope?

ANN   Don't we always?

PAUL   I'll get mine. (crosses to his book bag and takes out a jump rope)

ANN   (to MIKE) Are you sure you don't want to play with us? We'll show you what to do.

MIKE   Boys don't jump rope.

PAUL   I'm a boy and I jump rope.

MIKE   Only sissies jump rope.

ANN   That is, like, so not true. We are serious rope jumpers.

MIKE   Well, it's not a sport.

NICOLE   Oh, yeah, well, we're practicing up for a citywide competition.

PAUL   We'll let you join the team … if you think you've got what it takes.

MIKE   Oh, yeah? What does it take?

ANN   Ya gotta count—

NICOLE   Swing two ropes and remember the song—

PAUL   And of course you gotta jump!

NICOLE   Can you do three things at once?

MIKE   I can do anything girls can do.

NICOLE   Then join us!

MIKE   Forget it.

PAUL   There's nothing to be afraid of.

MIKE   I'm not afraid.

ANN   We won't laugh at you.

MIKE   You, laugh at me?! (sarcastically) I'm soooo scared!

PAUL   Come on. You made me catch that football.

MIKE   (blurts out) And you never did, did you? Because you're a fag! A loser! You're all losers! Rope-skipping, sissy, queer boy, fag LOSERS!* (stays in PAUL's face, taunting)

(MIKE's vicious outburst is followed by a stunned, hurt-filled silence.)

NICOLE   Come on, Paul, just ignore him.

PAUL   Okay. I guess you're right.

NICOLE   (to PAUL) You take the other end. Here. (PAUL and NICOLE extend two ropes between them. MIKE watches them) Go away, Mike. We don't want you here anymore.

MIKE   I can stand anywhere I want to.

NICOLE   Suit yourself. (glares at him)

PAUL   Just leave him alone, Nicole. Swing the rope!

(They begin to swing the ropes double Dutch style. MIKE watches them, amazed at their agility. ANN jumps into the ropes. They are real experts and get faster and faster while singing their chant in rhythm. As if they were practicing a dance routine, ANN steps out and takes the ropes from NICOLE, who then steps in. After a few lines, she too steps out and takes the ropes from PAUL, who then steps in.)

PAUL, NICOLE and ANN
        A-B-C,
        Easy as 1-2-3!
        My mama's on MTV.
        Baby you and me!
        Ooh, I—Got a piece of pie;
        Pie too sweet—want a piece of meat;
        Meat too tough—want to ride the bus;
        Bus too full—want to ride a bull;
        Bull attack—want my money back;
        Money too green—want a jelly bean;
        Jelly bean not cooked—want to write a
            book;
        Book not read—want to go to bed;
        Bed not made—want some lemonade;
        Lemonade too sour—we got pucker power!
        (the jumpers blow a kiss)

(Before they get to "Lemonade," PAUL gestures to MIKE to join them, and MIKE jumps in. Then he gets disoriented and tangled in the ropes: "WHOA!" He brings everyone down to the ground with him as he falls. They all laugh.)

MIKE   You guys are pretty good at this. I bet you win that competition.

NICOLE   I told you. We practice.

ANN   It's not as easy as it looks.

MIKE   You can say that again.

PAUL   Want to play with us after lunch?

MIKE   I don't know …

PAUL   Come on …

MIKE   I thought you hated me 'cuz I said all that stuff about you being fags** and losers.

NICOLE   Well, that wasn't very cool.

MIKE   I'm sorry. I was being a jerk.

(NICOLE, PAUL and ANN huddle.)

NICOLE, PAUL and ANN   Apology accepted!

PAUL   But see, what really matters is that I tried your game and you tried ours.

ANN   And we all fell down!

(The bell rings.)

NICOLE   Come you guys! We're gonna be late! (ANN and NICOLE rush off to their class hand-in-hand) 'Bye!

PAUL   Hey! I almost forgot my stuff! *(MIKE hands him his things)* Hey! Maybe after lunch, you can show me how to score a touchdown.

(PAUL hands MIKE his ball.)

MIKE   You're on! See you then! *(rushes off)*

PAUL   *(shouts to MIKE before running off in the opposite direction)* I bet we make it to the Super Bowl! *(exits)*

* *When performing* Anyone for Double Dutch? *for children younger than third grade, it is best to change this line to: "And you never did, did you? Because you're a sissy! A loser! You're all losers! Rope-skipping, sissy, queer boy LOSERS!"*

** *When performing* Anyone for Double Dutch? *for children younger than third grade, it is best to change this line to: "I thought you hated me 'cuz I said all that stuff about you being sissies and losers."*

Art by: (p.61) Betty Villalobos, PS#1, 6th Grade; (p.62) Helen Shen, Clover Avenue Elementary, 4th Grade; (p.63, top) Pilar Lopez, Canfield Elementary, 4th Grade, (bottom) Sosseh Taimoorian, Thomas Jefferson Elementary School, 4th Grade; (p.64) Naniqui Bernardez, Open Charter School, 2nd Grade

64

SNOOTY PATOOTY

by Mark E. Rosenthal and Carl Andress

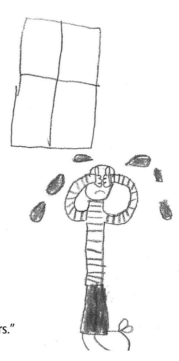

Snooty Patooty, nose in the air,
Snooty Patooty, just didn't care
About other folks' feelings—he needed no reason
To start with the name-calling and really mean teasin'!

Snooty Patooty called fat people "whales"
And said when they stepped on them they "broke the scales."
Snooty Patooty called black people "nappy!"
He'd say, "Scratch a record and make with the rappy!"
He called white people "honkies" and Latin folks "beaners!"
He said that poor kids ate nothing but "white bread and wieners."

If a girl wore glasses, he'd yell out, "Hey, four eyes!"
And he liked to call short people "midgets and small fries."
If you were a boy who couldn't play tag,
He'd laugh and he'd point and he'd call you a "fag."
"Big Nose" and "Jew Boy" he named Tommy Finkle,
And, "You're a gross lezzie!" he said to Kay Winkle.

Snooty Patooty, that big nose in the air,
Snooty Patooty, a walking nightmare!
'Til one day the new kid at school, Jenny Moody,
Finally met up with nasty old Snooty.
He took just one look and let out a sly snicker,
And said that she looked like a "big ol' nose picker!"

Well, Jenny just stared with a mad look on her face
And she put Mister Snooty right back in his place!
"You rant and you rave and you cause so much grief,
If you'd clean up your act we'd get some relief.
Look, if all you can see is 'black, fat or gay,'
You'll find you're alone at the end of the day.
No one enjoys being called 'this or that,'
All those awful words should be stuffed in your hat!
How would you feel if we picked on your clothes,
Or your weight or your race or the size of your NOSE!?"

Jenny reached out and grabbed him and hugged him real tight,
And whispered, "I know, deep down, you're really all right.
You're a little confused (and way off the track),
But with a bit of hard work, you'll find your way back!"
Well, Snooty, so shocked by all she had said,
Felt all of the insults fly out of his head.
He said, "Gosh, you're right! and I just want to say:
I'm terribly sorry for acting that way."

So, Snooty, he took his nose down from the air,
And Snooty Patooty learned how to care.
Thanks to Jennifer Moody, he now found a reason
To stop with the name-calling and really mean teasin'!!

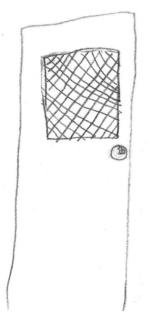

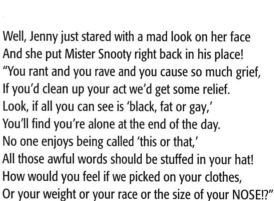

Art by Alex Fink, Crossroads School, 3rd Grade

THAT RACE PLACE

by Alice Tuan

The corner of Sunset Boulevard and Portia Avenue in Echo Park, Los Angeles. There is a bus stop sign.

MANNY, an African-American man, enters with a white cane. He carries a white plastic bag. After a few steps he turns to the audience. He listens to the street sounds.

MANNY   I know this street. I can't see, but I know this street. I feel my way down the street. Better yet, I smell my way down the street. Who says eyes was everything? See, I get off the bus at Echo Park Avenue. That lets me off right in front of the Pioneer Market here on Sunset Boulevard. You know it from the ladies selling their corn … you know they slather the cobs up with mayo and Squeeze Parkay, juice a little lemon on it and then roll it in flaked cheese, add a little chili powder … eat that thing off the stick. Do I got any mayo on my cheek? *(MANNY wipes his cheek)*

     But the real reason I'm down this way is the A-1 Supermarket—Oriental food warehouse … best prices around. You can get fresh fish, shrimp, crab, and they even have a butcher counter … someone actually cuts your meat the way you want it … But, I don't really go in there by myself 'cuz those Orientals get as aggressive with their shopping carts as they do with their cars … But, then next to that is their BBQ food store … MMM-mmm, you can smell the fried rice and the stewing pigs feet and the greens and fried chicken wings! But I … I get me some roasted duck. I know it's kinda fat, but every once in a while, I gotta get me half a duck to put on my noodles.

(MANNY shows the audience his bag.)

     You say this looks like more than half a duck? Well, it is. I got me a whole one 'cuz … I thought I'd give half to Lupe … her and her old man had another screaming match last night. She gets to squeakin' and cryin' … just breaks my heart. They live next door. Walls these days, thin as cardboard. Thought I'd take them duck … You know how food gets to be the family glue, you know? Oh, I hear the bus … You know those squeaky brakes? Won't rush for that one. I'll cross and wait with my whole duck for the next one no prob'.

(LANEY, an Asian-American girl with a steering wheel, appears upstage. She makes a manic turn and stops right before the crosswalk where MANNY is crossing.)

LANEY   I'm late! I'm late again! Shoot. C'mon, c'mon, c'mon.

(MANNY crosses slowly and Laney gets more frantic.)

     This guy's got all the time in the world! C'mon, man, c'mon!

(MANNY finishes crossing, waits at the bus stop. LANEY starts to turn left, stops, turns to audience:)

     Dig dang it! I forgot my notebook! I'm gonna be even later now!

(She makes a U-turn, heads back upstage from where she came.)

MANNY   That was some squeaking, peeling out wheels, changing directions just like that. Got me in a whirl just listening to it.

     (feels for the bus stop sign) Bus should be comin' up any minute now.

(LANEY enters again, even more frantic, right up to the edge of the stage, well into the crosswalk. She looks for oncoming traffic and doesn't see a Mexican-American woman, LUPE, entering, ready to cross the street.)

LUPE   These young people, always in a rush, in a rush. Don't even leave me no room to cross. *¡Soy la pedestriana*, I get to cross before the car!

(LANEY moves up ready to turn and almost bumps into LUPE.)

LANEY	Sorry, lady. I'm sorry.
LUPE	*(turning around)* Why don't you open up your Chink eyes.
LANEY	Hey, lady, no need to go there.
LUPE	*(putting her thumb and forefinger to her eye, as if opening it)* Open! Open your Chink eyes!
LANEY	Hey, no need to go to that race place.
LUPE	You no let me cross. You no see me.
LANEY	I already said I'm sorry. It's not like I did it on purpose!
LUPE	*(gesturing again)* Open! Open!
LANEY	*(pulling over)* It's not because of my eyes.
LUPE	*(squeaky) ¡Si!*
LANEY	No!
MANNY	Lupe, is that you?
LANEY	*(super fast)* Lady, I know I'm a careless driver sometimes! You can make me feel bad about not seeing you, but don't blame it on my race, don't go to that race place.
LUPE	*¿Qué dices, chinita? Hablas muy rápido.*
MANNY	It is you, isn't it, Lupe?
LANEY	*(to MANNY)* Sir, do you speak Spanish?
MANNY	A little.
LUPE	Meester Manny, she has Chink eyes, she almost kill me.
LANEY	Will you please, PLEASE, stop saying, "Chink"!?
LUPE	Chink, Chink, Chink, Chink, CHINK! Eyes so small!
LANEY	I'M SORRY! Do you understand that? I'M SORRY!
LUPE	*¿Por qué* you screaming at me?
MANNY	You gotta watch for us folk.
LANEY	I'm sorry. But, I'm human. I make mistakes.
MANNY	You people don't look. I almost got hit a couple of times.
LANEY	But what about all the times you *didn't* almost get hit when there was an Asian person driving? Or how many times do you almost get hit and it's *not* an Asian person driving. I mean, how do you even know, sir?
LUPE	Chink eyes.
LANEY	Okay, lady. I don't know what's up with you in your life that you can't grant me a little bit of forgiveness … Does your lashing out at me make you feel better?! *(trying to calm herself, starting to cry)* I'm hurt. I'm angry. And I'm looking up to the sky to give me the strength to understand that maybe, inside your heart you are even more hurt and more angry. But, someone's gotta stop this name-calling that hurts others for no reason. Do you understand what I'm saying?!

(Silence. LANEY gets back into her car and drives away.)

| LUPE | She talk too much. Talk too fast. |
| MANNY | She sure didn't sound Oriental. I'd never have known. |

LUPE	What she say?
MANNY	*(slowly, trying to be clear)* She say maybe you angry about something else, not her.

(Pause.)

LUPE	Ah, Meester Manny … I can for you take one dollar for bus?
MANNY	You need a dollar for the bus?
LUPE	My husband drink … all money gone.

(Pause.)

MANNY	Yeah, I got a buck.

(He hands her a dollar. Beat.)

	Hey, Lupe, you like duck?
LUPE	*¿Qué es duck?*
MANNY	*(shows plastic bag)* In here. Quack, quack, quack! Quack, quack—
LUPE	*¡Pato!*
MANNY	Duck. You like?
LUPE	*(sniffing) ¡Delicioso!*
MANNY	Duck.
LUPE	Dook.
MANNY	Quack, quack, quack!
LUPE	Quack, quack, quack!
MANNY and LUPE	Quack, quack, quack!

(Lights fade as we hear the bus approach with its squeaky wheels.)

MARIPOSAS

by Miguel Lopez with Pamela Weymouth

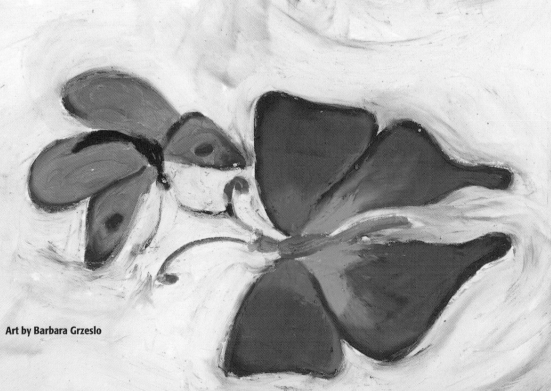

Every day at school they call me, "Girlie, sissy, gaylord, *mariposa*!"
I wish there was a world of *mariposas* … butterflies,
Where everyone could be free,
Without being tormented, teased and threatened—
A world without hate.
Un mundo full of butterflies—red and blue, yellow, green, pink and orange!
A world where however you look:
Big or small, dark or light,
You would be treated the same—
Con amor y respeto—
As every creature deserves to be!

My world, outside this galaxy,
Inside my *corazón*,
Is open to everybody,
Without judgment.

Mi mundo de mariposas
Is a place where I can be me.

Art by Barbara Grzeslo

BE PROUD OF YOUR DIFFERENCE!

Art by Lemond Harris, Cragmont Elementary, 1st Grade

BE PROUD

BIANCA LAGUNAS: "I like to talk to my imaginary friends."

DONALD W. MOSS, JR.: "My bald spot is special!"

LATEAREA TATUM: "I feel good because I am little."

OF YOUR DIFFERENCE!

MONIQUE WILLIAMSON: "I'd like to be a doctor so I can help people."

DAVID LEE: "I like to study and do 1, 2, 3's up to 1,000,000,000!"

SHEENA RICE: "I like to learn about things I did not know before."

JOSHUA ROMERO: "I'm different because I'm mixed."

3rd Grade Students from Nora Sterry Elementary School, Los Angeles, Arlene Karon (teacher) and Anna Marie Fierro (assistant teacher)

MICHAEL CARPIO: "I want to be an artist."

LEVI MOCK: "Don't listen to the people who pick on you. And follow your dreams."

GEORGETTE TOWNSON: "I want to be a mermaid because I won't have to take a bath!"

YASMIN ANTONIO: "Don't think you're weird, your difference is special!"

CHRISTIAN M. RAY: "I am unique because I am little and I can do my work good."

PRENTISS WESTBROOKS: "I like to do back flips."

Ms. Arlene Karon, Ms. Anna Marie Fierro

MOTHER NATURE

by Nancy Alicia de Los Santos

MOTHER NATURE enters singing. She's a beautiful woman, though she seems slightly off-center. She is dressed in a flowing, chiffon, formal-length gown, topped off with a wild and crazy headpiece that has the solar system twirling around it. Pee-Wee Herman would kill for it! Over her dress she wears a patchwork-quilt apron with faces of different types of people—girls, boys, men, women, with white skin, black skin, yellow skin, etc. She carries a huge wooden bowl and spoon. She's happy and dances while she works. "Shortenin' Bread" plays under the scene.

MOTHER *(singing and mixing cookie dough)*:

Mama's little babies love shortenin', shortenin'!
Mama's little babies love shortenin' bread!"

(Notices the audience.)

OH! Oh my, oh my, oh my! I didn't know I was having company today. But then again, you're always welcome at Mother Nature's house! Oh, my goodness! I remember every single one of you. Oh, you don't remember me … You were each just a teeny weeny little bitty thought when I knew you! The recipe for every single one of you started right here—in this here bowl!

(She surveys the crowd, selects a child from the audience, gets him up on stage. To the child:)

You! Stand up, son. Stand up tall! Don't slouch! I planned for you to be … *(describes the child's hair color, eye color, dimples, etc.)* I planned for you to be handsome, intelligent and kindhearted. I used chocolate chips for your eyes, and wheat flour for your hair, and a big gallon of sweet, sweet honey to make your heart kind and loving to dogs and cats and elephants! *(to the children in the audience)* Did it work? *(encourages children in audience to agree)*

(aside, to child) You don't know it yet, but in the future, you'll be working with elephants! Details later. Much later!

(Again, she checks out the children in the audience.)

I did a pretty good job on you all!
You're a good-looking batch of people!

(She points to another child.)

Hey, I remember you. Look! You look exactly like I thought you would. Hair the color of licorice, little stars in your eyes! Beautiful! Just beautiful!

(Then to all the children in the audience:)

Now, even though he's got chocolate-chip eyes, and she's got licorice hair *(points to a new child)* and you've got cherry cheeks, I used the same basic recipe for you all: LOVE! And that's why, deep down inside—right at the very, very center of our hearts and souls—we are all the same. So, though everyone's totally different on the outside, everyone's exactly the same inside—*plumb full* of sweet LOVE! Just like cookies! We're all different colors and shapes and sizes—some are big and some are small, some are sprinkly and some are spicy! Some speak Spanish, some Chinese. Some like to dance, some like to play sports, some are rich, some are poor, some are old, some are young, some are gay, some are straight, some are Muslim, some Jewish, some like to read and write, and some like to do math! Like I always say: "Variety is the spice of life!"

Laura Nagata Murphy (*Cootie Shots* cast member) with audience member, Caitlyn Higa

Costume design and rendering by Martha Ferrara

IT TAKES ALL KINDS

Lyrics by Mark Waldrop, music by Brad Ellis

Music on page 143

(Sung:)

Mother Nature's pretty smart and she always finds
That she likes variety: it takes all kinds.
Do you like a peach's fuzzy skin or smooth watermelon rinds?
Both are lovely to the touch: it takes all kinds!

What good would a rainbow be if it were only blue?
What if ev'ryone you met was a clone of you? Oooh!

(Spoken:)

That's why they put different flavor LifeSavers in the pack, man,
So life don't get too boring!

(Sung:)

Some creatures run or jump or fly, some sit on their behinds;
Fast or slow, they go to show: it takes all kinds!

(Spoken:)

Let me give you another example:

(Sung:)

Look at little Emily: frilly dress and Barbie dolls;
Check out little Betty Sue: Tonka trucks and overalls.
No one's wrong and no one's right, ev'rything is fine, you see—
Each of them is beautiful being who she wants to be.

William is a whiz at sports, rough and tumble, tough as nails;
Tom spends ev'ry afternoon practicing his piano scales.
Diff'rent boys with diff'rent gifts—which is better his or his?
Mother Nature loves them both: each true to who he is.

Diff'rent styles and diff'rent smiles, diff'rent hearts and minds,
Make the world a richer place, make a better human race—
Here's a concept to embrace: it takes all kinds!

Art by Albert Llanos, Cragmont Elementary, 2nd Grade

OPPOSITION

by Tony Kushner

The universe exists because of opposites and tension,

A fact we sometimes overlook, but here deserves a mention.

For every action there's another action to oppose it:

It's common sense, for life is tense, and everybody knows it.

Inside the heart of every star there's thermonuclear fission

Resulting from a constant state of atoms in collision.

Hydrogen to helium, a force that pushes out:

Ten Billion Years Of Blowing Up is what a star's about.

The star could not exist, it would be blown to smithereens,

With so much inside pushing out, lest something intervenes.

And something does, for pulling in is gravity, of course,

Which does the trick of holding in the thermonuclear force.

So one force pushes out, while one is pulling in,

And let's all thank our lucky stars that neither one can win!

For when the tension ceases, and the totter doesn't teeter,

We'll all be painfully aware we've lost our solar heater—

We will either freeze to death or get blown to Jehovah,

Depending if the sun becomes a black hole or a nova.

And on that day I'm sad to say all life abruptly stops;

But there's five billion years before it shrivels or it pops.

So don't despair; instead reflect upon the stellar state

And on the fundamental fact that stars illuminate.

From grains of sand to giant stars all things share one condition:

The world we see would never be, except for opposition.

CHOCOLATE FACE

by Cynthia Ruffin

Chocolate Face! That's ME!
From the top of my head,
To the tips of my toes,
Chocolate all.

Brown like Cocoa and Chocolate Easter Bunnies,
Yum-yum, that's me.

Or Caramel-Colored,
Or Black as licorice,
Or Cool Tan like coffee with just a drop of cream.

Chocolate Face. Me, me, me.
Brown like a magnolia tree.
Tan like King Tut
Or
Blue-Black like a cloudless midnight sky.
All, ALL, ME.

Chocolate Face with Chocolate Eyes
And Chocolate Lips that grin real wide
When Mommy pinches my perfect
Peanut Butter–colored cheeks. Mmmm.

Shiny like the golden sun,
Running free, having fun.
Yummy like a pan of fudge,
Eat so much that I can't budge.

Chocolate ME, from head to foot—
I'm chocolate through and through,
It's true.
Not everyone likes Chocolate's taste,
But I'll always love my Chocolate Face.

Art by Peter Brooke

AT YOUR AGE?!

by Bea Bernstein

The sound of a motorcycle is heard from offstage.

MAN *(from offstage)* HEY! WATCH IT, GRANDMA!

BEA *(enters wearing a leather jacket and carrying a helmet)* Watch where you're walkin', bub! *(to audience)* Grandma?! I should be so lucky. They see white hair on a motorcycle, suddenly I have grandchildren?

MALCOLM *(enters, wearing a leather jacket)* Hey, Grandma! How about giving me a ride on your bike?

BEA Get away from me, kid. Ya bother me.

MALCOLM Don't call me "kid."

BEA Don't call me "Grandma."

MALCOLM Sorry, I thought all old ladies liked to be called "Grandma."

BEA Not this one. "*Old lady*" is not so hot, either. My name's Bea.

MALCOLM Nice to meet you, Bea. I'm Malcolm. *(they shake hands)* I've never seen an old … er, a grand … um. Way to ride that bike!

Art by Adan Valdez

BEA	Thanks, Malcolm. Years of practice.
MALCOLM	Why don't you like being called "Grandma"?
BEA	'Cuz I don't have grandchildren, for one. And 'cuz people usually call me that when they're trying to say I'm too old for something.
MALCOLM	That's *exactly* how I feel about people calling me "kid." They say "kid," but what they mean is … well … I'm too young to think for myself.
BEA	And people think I'm too *old* to think for myself.
MALCOLM	They think you don't matter as much 'cuz of your age?
BEA	Exactly. No respect.

(Pause.)

MALCOLM	I like your jacket.
BEA	I like yours, too. Wanna know a secret?
MALCOLM	Always!
BEA	My daughter *hates* it when I wear this jacket. She thinks I'm trying to pretend I'm a teenager. She'd rather I wore frilly dresses and hats? Feh! Let me tell ya–hats and motorcycles don't mix.
MALCOLM	I know! My mom feels the same way about my jacket! She thinks I'm trying to look like a teenager. She says this jacket is gonna make me grow up too fast.
BEA	You know, come to think of it, we have a lot in common.
MALCOLM	I guess we do. Do people ever talk about you like you're not even there?
BEA	Uch! Are you kidding? All the time!

(Scene shift: BEA is seated with her son DAVID and his wife MICHELLE at their dinner table.)

DAVID	Was she okay today?
MICHELLE	How do I know? All she ever does is ride the *meshuggenah* motorbike.
DAVID	She looks all right.
BEA	Hello! I can still hear and speak! Does anyone want to ask *me* how I feel!?

(Pause.)

MICHELLE	She's a little over tired.
DAVID	She probably needs a nap.

(BEA returns to the scene with MALCOLM.)

BEA	See what I mean?
MALCOLM	It sorta reminds me of dinner at my house.

(Scene shift: MALCOLM eats dinner with his parents and his older brother.)

DAD	I don't know who taught your son to say such words!
MOM	Well, I'm not surprised. He doesn't have enough to do with his free time.
DAD	We have a lawn, don't we?

(MALCOLM's brother makes faces at him.)

MALCOLM	*(to BROTHER)* CUT IT OUT!
MOM and DAD	What?!!
MALCOLM	He's teasing me!
MOM	Not this again.
DAD	Go to your room and don't come out until you're grown-up enough to ignore your brother.

(The BROTHER continues making faces)

MALCOLM	He's doing it AGAIN!

(MOM and DAD turn to look, but the BROTHER puts on an innocent "What, me?" face.)

DAD	He gets this from your side of the family.
MOM	No, he doesn't.

(MALCOLM returns to the scene with BEA.)

BEA	It doesn't seem fair.
MALCOLM	What?
BEA	People use our age as a reason not to listen to us.
MALCOLM	Yeah. *(pause)* But, y'know what reeeeeally makes me angry!?
BEA	What?
MALCOLM	Getting laughed at for liking things I'm not supposed to like "at my age."
BEA	You're tellin' me!

MALCOLM	Yeah! Like, for instance, I like to play shuffleboard and … I like to rock.
BEA	That's not so unusual! *(demonstrates a dance move)* Everybody likes to rock!
MALCOLM	In a rocking chair?
BEA	*(guffaws)* Come again?
MALCOLM	*(a little hurt)* I like to rock in a rocking chair. I find it soothing.
BEA	Oh. Well, better you than me. Y'know what I find soothing?
MALCOLM	What.
BEA	*(whispers)* My Sony PlayStation. *(or substitute this with the current most popular electronic game)*
MALCOLM	*(bursts out)* YOU'VE GOT A PLAYSTATION!?
BEA	Not so loud! Everyone will want to play.
MALCOLM	I've never understood those things.

BEA	It takes practice.
MALCOLM	Would you show me how?
BEA	I guess I could. But, I get to be Wolverine! *(see note in dialogue above regarding PlayStation)*
MALCOLM	Cool.

(They start to exit.)

BEA	So, this shuffleboard? Is it hard?
MALCOLM	It's easy … I'll show ya!
BEA	Promise you won't laugh?
MALCOLM	As long as you promise not to laugh at me when I lose on the PlayStation.
BEA	Deal.

(BEA and MALCOLM exchange high fives and exit.)

BRIGHT ORANGE FINGERNAILS

by Mark E. Rosenthal, based on a true story by Joan Atkinson, developed through improvisation with Fringe Benefits

RODNEY gives a class report as if the audience were the class.

RODNEY   "My Hero," by Rodney Samson:

A few years ago, when I was in pre-school, we would spend a whole week on each letter of the alphabet. During that week, we'd bring in stuff that began with that letter. Like for "A" week, we brought in apples and art. And all of our activities that week had something to do with the magic letter "A." For "N" week, we had noodles and Now and Laters and played with NASCAR racers, and Nintendo, and talked about Nickelodeon. (We couldn't *watch* it 'cuz we didn't have cable in school.) We also painted our nails, 'cuz "nails" starts with the letter "N." It was really fun! Rachel painted each of her nails a different color, and Tommy painted his nails red, white and blue, and Janie Chang painted hers with polka dots! I chose bright orange, 'cuz it's the color of Tigger.

I couldn't wait for school to be over so I could go to Scouts and show everyone how neat my nails looked. Then my dad showed up …

(Back in pre-school.)

DAD   Ready for the Cub Scouts meeting, sport?

RODNEY   Yeah! I can't wait till they see what I did in class today! *(shows DAD his nails, then to audience)* I got the feeling my dad wasn't happy with what I had done.

DAD   *(color has drained from his face)* Whatcha got there, Rodney?

RODNEY   They're orange, Daddy! See! And they sparkle when I move 'em around like this … *(holds his hands up directly in front of DAD's face and waves them around)*

DAD   *(gently takes his son's hands and tries to hide them)* Um … that's real … nice, slugger. *(calls out to teacher)* Ms. Garza? Um, could I have a word with you, please?

Ms. Garza	Rodney, have you shown your father what a nice job you did on your nails?
Rodney	YES!! *(wrestles away and waves his hands in front of Dad's face)* Sparkly! See!
Dad	Rodney, why don't you go get your stuff? You don't want to be late for the camp out.
Rodney	Okay! *(runs off)*
Dad	Ms. Garza, why is Rodney wearing nail polish?
Ms. Garza	Well, all of the children are. It's "N" week, remember? We did send home that permission slip.
Dad	Oh, that? I thought only the girls would be doing that. *(pause)* Do you have anything to take it off?
Ms. Garza	Yes, we do.
Dad	Thank goodness! I couldn't begin to think of a way to explain this to the other Scouts. May I have the polish remover?
Ms. Garza	I already asked Rodney if he wanted to take it off. He said no.
Dad	Well, we'll see about that. Rodney?
Rodney	Yes?
Dad	Don't you think you'd feel better if we took that nail polish off before—
Rodney	NOOOOOOOOO! I LIKE IT AND I WANT TO KEEP IT!
Dad	Okay. But, what if the other boys make fun of you? They might not understand.
Rodney	Then, I'll explain it to them. Maybe I can borrow some nail polish and show them. Can I, Ms. Garza?!
Dad	Rodney, some people think only girls wear nail polish.
Rodney	But, that's not true. 'Cuz I'm wearing it, and so is Tommy, and so is Mike!
Dad	I mean, they think that if you wear nail polish … well … um …
Rodney	What?
Dad	They think … um … It's kinda hard to explain.
Rodney	They don't think it makes you a girl, do they? 'Cuz that would be really dumb! I'm still Rodney. Just … now I have BRIGHT ORANGE FINGERNAILS!!
Dad	We're going to be late. Let's just sit down and clean this nail polish off and—
Rodney	NO!!!
Dad	Rodney, listen—
Rodney	NO! I'm not gonna take it off!

(Pause. Dad studies Rodney and sighs deeply.)

Dad	Okay, then, you're leaving me no choice. This is going to hurt me more than it hurts you—
Ms. Garza	Mr. Samson!
Dad	My mind is made up, Ms. Garza. If my son is going to Scout Camp wearing orange nail polish … then so am I! …

(Rodney continues his report:)

Rodney	And, we even painted our toenails together! That was the most amazing day ever! We had so much fun at Scout Camp. And when we got home and showed my mom, she just laughed and laughed. When my dad asked why she was laughing, she said: "Like father, like son!" I guess that isn't so bad.

STUDENT TEACHERS

by Jehan F. Agrama

ANJOUM (Ahn-joom), a twelve-year-old girl, kneels with her forehead on the floor. She is getting up, after finishing her prayer, just as her classmate, NECIE (Nee-cee), comes in.

NECIE   Oh, I'm sorry, Anjoum, I thought the classroom was empty.

ANJOUM   That's okay, Necie.

NECIE   What were you doing kneeling on the floor?

ANJOUM   I was praying.

NECIE   Yes, but you had your head on the ground and I've never seen anyone pray like that before.

ANJOUM   Well, I'm a Muslim, and when we pray, we look up to God, but we also bow down and kneel down to give thanks to God. *(demonstrates all three postures: standing with hands cupping sides of head, hands on knees bent forward, and kneeling with forehead touching ground)*

NECIE   I heard Muslims pray all day long? Is that true?

ANJOUM   Sometimes it feels like it, but it's once before the sun rises, once in the morning, once in the afternoon, once as the sun sets and once before we go to bed. It's five times in all and it's really not that long. Besides, it helps me remember to keep God in my life.

NECIE   What exactly do Muslims believe? Is it called Muslimism?

ANJOUM   Our religion is actually called Islam. Our main belief is that there is one God, Allah, and that Muhammad is his prophet. We say that every day in our prayers. There are four other things you must do in Islam: prayer (five times each day), fasting, giving charity and *Hajj* (or pilgrimage to Mecca, our holy place).

NECIE   You've told me why you pray, and I think that helping poor people is also very important, but why do you fast?

ANJOUM   Well, during *Ramadan (Ra-ma-dahn)*, our holy month, we fast so we can concentrate on our love and need for Allah. Fasting teaches us self-discipline and also makes us feel a greater sympathy for the poor. Ramadan lasts twenty-eight days.

NECIE   You mean you don't eat for a whole month!

ANJOUM   Well, first of all, not everyone fasts. If you're pregnant, very little, very old or sick, you don't, because it wouldn't be healthy. And, we only fast during daylight. So, we get up before the sun comes up and have breakfast and then we get to stay up very late to have dinner. This is usually a time that we have friends and family over, and we love staying up late. Also, getting up in the dark can be fun. It feels special!

NECIE   That sounds neat. Maybe I could try it with you sometime.

ANJOUM   I'm sure my parents would invite you to break the fast with us. You could come very early, have *Fitar (Fi-tahr)* with us one morning, or you could join us for *Sohur (So-hoor)* late at night and sleep over.

NECIE   Hey "break the fast"! That must be where we got "breakfast" from!

ANJOUM   Maybe you're right. I never thought about that.

NECIE   I would love to break the fast with you! That would be great! Hey, are you fasting now?

ANJOUM   No. Wanna go get a Coke?

NECIE   Well, I can't drink Coke, but I'll have a Sprite.

ANJOUM   Cool. *(they start out the door, then)* Why can't you drink Coke?

NECIE   It's a long story.

ANJOUM   We've got ten minutes 'til class starts.

NECIE   Okay. Well, I'm Mormon. We don't drink caffeine. It all goes back to …

(They exit.)

IN MOMMY'S HIGH HEELS

Lyrics by Paul Selig, music by Scott Killian

Music on page 145

*A young boy is on his knees, or sitting at his school desk,
alone on stage. It is important that the audience not see his shoes.*

Yesterday at show-and-tell
The other kids began to yell!
What could have caused this wild and crazy scene?

It wasn't Joey's pet hyena,
The shrunken heads from Argentina,
The bumble bees that swarmed around
When Cassie dropped their hive.

It wasn't Mary's puppy Chuck
That got hit by the garbage truck;
She got a shovel, dug him up,
For all the world to see.

It wasn't Alfred's mustard plaster;
The Eskimos from Nome, Alaska,
Who told us of their blubber diet,
That caused my class to shriek and riot.

It wasn't Frieda's brother Fred,
Who has six noses and three heads,
Or Tommy's mommy's kidney stones
That floated in a jar.

It wasn't Leo's model cars,
The Campbell twins' appendix scars
That caused my class to hiss and boo
And shriek and wail and scream.

Who knew when it would come my turn,
Their jaws would drop, my cheeks would burn?
I'm standing there for all the world to see.

I didn't bring a thing to share,
I only brought two things I wear
That make me happy, make me tall.
They can laugh, but I'm above them all—

(He stands, revealing himself to be wearing high heels.)

In Mommy's high heels the world is beautiful,
Let the peasants choke way down below.
I'm standing high above the crowds,
My head is breaking through the clouds.
In Mommy's high heels I'm ten feet tall!

In Mommy's high heels life's a fantasy:
Ev'ry wish I make is a decree!
Let Sissy keep her shrunken heads,
Let Mary walk her dog who's dead.
In my mommy's high heels I have it all!

Here the world is beautiful:
Forests of coat racks and shoe trees,
A land of hope and shopping sprees!
When I grow up, I'll have the cash
To go and buy a bag to match!

*(Soft-shoe dance break, possibly with spoken phrases
from the lyrics.)*

So let them say I'm like a girl!
What's wrong with being like a girl?!
And let them jump and jeer and whirl—
They are the swine, I am the pearl!
And let them laugh and let them scream!
They'll be beheaded when I'm queen!
When I rule the world! When I rule the world!
When I rule the world, in my mommy's high heels!

Shoe of the evening, beautiful shoe.

Any one for shoes?

I dream of Jeannie with the light brown shoes.

Andy Warhol

Beauty is shoe, shoe beauty.

Uncle Sam wants Shoe!

You can lead a shoe to water but you can't make it drink.

Shoe bright, shoe light, first shoe I've seen tonight

When I'm Calling Shoe.

Art by Andy Warhol

The autobiography of Alice B. shoe.

89

MOVING

Y'know, it seems like since the world began,
Folks have been fighting with other folks …
Calling them "abnormal" or "weird" just 'cuz they're different
In some way or other!

Everyone moves, right from the beginning;
But life's not a race, there's no losing or winning.
Movement gets us from right here to left there—
Walking or running, on foot or by chair,
Leaning forward or backward, looking up, straight or down,
Laughing or crying, with smile or frown.
The way that we get from point A to point Z,
Is not always like what we see on TV.

We lead with our hips! We walk on our toes!
Watch out for walls if you lead with your nose!
His big steps, her *huge* steps, my steps that are small …
So small that it seems I'm not moving at all!
Some walk like their parents, who taught them one day;
Some find it easier to make their own way.

Big feet or small feet, with ten toes or eight,
We all get around with our own special gait.
Gait is a word to describe how you walk,
And *pitch* is a word to describe how you talk.
We each have a *pitch*, and we each have a *gait*
That's comfortable to us, we call that a *trait*.
Trait is a word to describe what you're made of;
If we were like marbles, they're what we'd make trades of.

"I'll trade you my brown eyes, for your green ones—there!"
"I'll trade you my big butt, for her long black hair!"
Changing your traits is possible too:
"I can make my voice higher or dye my hair blue!"
"I can walk like an elephant or talk like a duck!"
"I can make myself giggle when I want to yuck yuck!"

90

The reasons we do this—try to change who we are—
Are not always simple, they don't come in a jar.
To fit in! To be cool! So they'll like you in school!
To not be the weird one is sometimes the rule.
To please Mommy or Daddy or teachers or friends:
We'll do what we have to! We'll go to all ends!
> 'Cuz these people love us and wish us the best,
> They don't want us teased or apart from the rest.

> "Only girls play with dollies!" "Only boys play with balls!"
> "Only girls sing soprano!" "Boys don't skip down the halls!"

> So, I walk like they say to and make my voice low,
> And sometimes I even forget it's for show.
> But if that walk hurts me and makes my legs sore,
> Or if using that voice has become just a chore,

Then I find myself faced with decisions to make:
Do I keep doing these things when they cause me to ache?!

Being your real self is not easy to do:
Does anyone else walk or talk like I do?
What if they laugh at me, call me bad names?
They won't let me play in their reindeer games!
> I'll tell you my friend—it's just my advice—
> Those people who'd tease you, they're not very nice!
> > Who wants to play with those creepy creeps!?
> > I want my friends to be friends for keeps!
> > And *if* they don't like how you walk or talk,
> > Then they're big ol' chickens, to them I say, "Braawk!!"
> > > 'Cuz they're all just *afraid* of DIFFERENCE, you see—
> > > And that's what makes you *you* and what makes me *me*!

> > > So, instead of feeling ugly, 'cuz when I walk I bounce,
> > > I should try to remember, it's being *me* that counts!
> > > The way that you move, the way that you talk,
> > > Your brown eyes, your big butt, your feelings and thoughts—
> > > All that I am and all I can be: ideas, plans and memories,
> > > They all make me *me*!
> > > So when you discover your own special *gait*,
> > > Or *pitch*, or *idea*, or *talent*, or *trait*,
> > > > Be *proud* of your difference! No need to feel bad!
> > > > You're the best *you* this world's ever had!
> > > > You're unique! You're special! You're way outta sight!
> > > > There are no mistakes—you turned out just right!

by Mark E. Rosenthal

SHE'S A REAL SPAZ

by John Belluso

For Callie Smartt

Art by Pirate Princess Poppy

A school yard. EMILY, a young girl with cerebral palsy, enters in her wheelchair. Her speech is a bit impaired and her legs spasm occasionally.

EMILY   *(to the audience)* So here I am, wheeling through the school yard one afternoon, trying to get up enough courage to talk to them—those girls.

(Cheerleading music plays. Three cheerleaders—JUSTINE, CHRISTINE and PRISTINE—enter, pom-poms in hand, strutting like supermodels. They begin practicing their cheers:)

JUSTINE, CHRISTINE and PRISTINE
          Yellowbutts—Yellowbutts—Yellowbutts—GO!
          We're gonna put on a really good SHOW!
          Our team's points are gonna add up and GROW!
          Yellowbutts—Yellowbutts—Yellowbutts—GO!

(They repeat this cheer as EMILY watches them adoringly. EMILY then begins moving her arms and legs, trying to imitate the cheerleaders' moves, yelling along with them. When the cheerleaders see her, they all stop their cheers. EMILY keeps cheering. She has a few spasms in her legs and her cheering slows down.)

EMILY   *(smiling)* Yellowbutts—Yellowbutts—

CHRISTINE   Excuse me, what are you doing?

(EMILY stops cheering.)

EMILY   My name's Emily.

CHRISTINE   Well, yes, I'm sure it is, but you see …

EMILY   What's your name?

CHRISTINE   *(presenting herself)* Well, since you asked, my name is Christine!

JUSTINE   *(also presenting herself, trying to top CHRISTINE's presentation)* And I'm Justine!

PRISTINE   *(also presenting herself, the most beautiful and fabulous presentation yet)* And I'm Pristine! And we are …

JUSTINE, CHRISTINE and PRISTINE   The Cheerleading Squad for the Fighting Yellowbutts football team!!!

PRISTINE   *(bending over, tapping EMILY on her nose condescendingly, speaking loudly)* You see, honey, we are cheeeeer-leeeaders! …

EMILY   Uh, yeah, I know that. *(to the audience)* The pom-poms were a dead giveaway.

PRISTINE   So, what can we do for you, dear?

EMILY   *(getting up her courage)* You see, I … I wanna join the cheerleading team.

(A long pause, she has a few more spasms in her legs.)

CHRISTINE   You what?

EMILY   I wanna join the team. I have a lot of school spirit and I can yell really, really loud and I can help paint signs and all the other stuff that cheerleaders do—I mean, I can't jump and do flips and move around exactly like you guys do, but I can move around in my own ways. I can dance! I dance all the time! *(a pause)* So, I wanna be a cheerleader.

(CHRISTINE looks to JUSTINE in horror. JUSTINE looks to PRISTINE in even greater horror. PRISTINE opens her eyes and her mouth very wide:)

PRISTINE   MOTHER!!!!

(PRISTINE'S MOTHER enters grandly. Her eyes and her nose are constantly pointing upward, so she doesn't even see EMILY sitting in her wheelchair.)

MOTHER   Yes, my precious milkchocolatechipoatmealraisincookie of a daughter, what is the problem?

PRISTINE   Mother, as the coach of our cheerleading team, we need your help. There is a … uh … girl here, who, uh, wants to join our team.

Mother   *(accidentally spitting in her daughter's face with every "s")* Oh, well, isn't that just smashing! We could use another spunky, spirited, little spitfire on our squad …

PRISTINE   *(wiping the spittle away)* Yes, but, uh, Mother, you don't seem to understand *(sotto voce)* this girl is not a spitfire … she is a spaz.

MOTHER   Now dear, you know how I feel about name-calling. It's not very dignified …

PRISTINE   No, Mother, I mean, she's a real spaz, she's like, spastic, she has spasms in her legs—look!

MOTHER   *(looking down, seeing EMILY for the first time, startled)* Oh! Dear! *(composing herself, bending down to EMILY)* Well, hello there, my little peanutbutterfluffanutterbuttercupcake, you just … you scared—I mean, you surprised me a little, that's all. How are you?

EMILY   I'm fine. *(to the audience)* This lady's hairdo scared me a little, so I guess we're even. *(back to MOTHER)* I wanna be a cheerleader, ma'am.

MOTHER   Yes, well, I'm sure you understand, that would simply not be possible!

EMILY   Why not?

(MOTHER looks to the other girls, and they egg her on.)

MOTHER   Well, well, I would think it would be … it would be an issue of safety—yes, safety! Suppose you got hit by a stray football? You'd be hurt.

EMILY   *(pointing)* Suppose one of them got hit by a stray football? They'd be hurt, too!

JUSTINE   *(thinking about it)* Gosh, I hope I don't get hit by a stray football. I don't wanna get hurt.

CHRISTINE   *(to JUSTINE)* You're not gonna get hit by a stray football!

EMILY   Then what makes you so sure I'll get hit by a stray football? Everybody takes chances in life, but you can't be afraid of taking chances—I'm not afraid!

MOTHER   Uh, yes, and you are certainly a plucky little pumpkinpeachprunecobbler, but I really do think …

EMILY   Besides, I mean, I may have cerebral palsy, but I'm still pretty strong, and I can dance—I dance all the time—and I really think it would be so much fun and a great way to make friends and …

MOTHER   *(clearing her throat, interrupting EMILY)* As the coach of the Fighting Yellowbutts Cheerleading Squad, I'm sure you understand—it would simply not be possible. *(gathering up the girls)* Now come along girls, it's time for us to head to the locker rooms! Away from here! Let's go! To the locker rooms! Away from here!

(MOTHER and the cheerleaders exit, except for JUSTINE, who stands behind EMILY, looking at her. EMILY looks up and sees JUSTINE.)

EMILY   *(indignantly)* What?

JUSTINE   *(looking away)* Nothing. I'm sorry if I was staring at you.

EMILY   You weren't staring at me, you were just looking at me.

JUSTINE   Oh yeah. *(a pause)* Hey, would you be mad if I asked you a question?

EMILY   Why would I be mad? I'm always asking people questions.

JUSTINE	Okay, well, that thing you said you had …
EMILY	*(interrupting)* Cerebral palsy. Don't worry, it's not contagious.
JUSTINE	*(a little angry)* I didn't think it was.
EMILY	*(looking up at her; pauses; then smiling, as if to say: "I'm sorry")* Oh. Okay. So, what's your question?

(EMILY's legs spasm a little. MOTHER can be heard, calling from offstage:)

MOTHER	JUSTIIIIIIINE … Where are you my little horseradishwhippedcreamtwoallbeefpattiesspecialsauceiccreamsundae!?!
JUSTINE	*(calling back to her)* I'll be along in a minute! *(back to EMILY, a bit nervous)* Well, I guess my question is really two questions.
EMILY	Okay, what's the first one?
JUSTINE	*(staring at the ground, very nervous)* Why, why do your legs shake like that?
EMILY	It's 'cuz of the cerebral palsy, it gives me spasms—but that doesn't mean I'm a spaz or nothin'; it just means my legs shake, that's all. It's really not that scary, you get used to it after a while.
JUSTINE	*(still staring at the ground)* Yeah.
EMILY	So what's your other question?
JUSTINE	*(sitting on a bench next to EMILY)* You said before … that you dance, that you like to dance …
EMILY	*(smiling)* Yeah, I do …
JUSTINE	Well, how do you, dance?
EMILY	I just move my body to the music, it's fun!

(Contemporary pop music plays.)

My mom says it's my own personal way of dancing. It's like this …

(EMILY moves and shifts to the beat of the music. JUSTINE is a little uncomfortable at this sight, but then slowly joins in with the dance, trying to dance EMILY's way, staying seated on the bench. EMILY's legs spasm a little, but the spasms blend in with the dance. JUSTINE tries to imitate the spasms as if they were just another part of the dance. They laugh and dance. EMILY, still dancing, wheels forward to address the audience:)

So I didn't get onto the cheerleading team this time, but there's always next year. And Justine's pretty cool. We eat lunch together a lot. *(smiling)* She's coming over to my house next Saturday night. My mom's going to take us dancing.

(EMILY returns to JUSTINE, and they continue dancing EMILY's way, as lights and music fade.)

THE PRINCESS PETUNIA

by Liz Carlisle

Once upon a time, in a faraway place,
Lived the Princess Petunia, blessed with beauty and grace.

She frolicked in the flowers 'til she heard of her fate:
To marry Prince Poppy, a wonderful mate.
Petunia liked Poppy, he was gentle and kind;
Her family thought him a wonderful find.
But she loved another, secret and true,
And the king, he knew nothing of this big to-do.
She had to tell him. She hoped he'd understand,
That she just couldn't bring herself to marry this man.

"Father," she said, "it makes me wince,
To think that I should marry this prince!"

"But why, my dear?" the king inquired,
"Do you think him too old and too tired?"

"No, no, Papa," Petunia confessed,
"The one I love … she wears a dress!
Her name is Violet, she's ever so pretty,
And none in the kingdom is near half as witty!"

The king grumbled and paced throughout the day,
"She'll never have sons or daughters this way!"

"Petunia," he said, in a harsh-sounding tone,
"This type of behavior I cannot condone."

So the princess ran crying out into the wood,
And to her dear Violet, who, of course, understood.

"Petunia, don't fear, don't shed one more tear:
A love great as ours is will not disappear!"

From his window on high, the king watched and sighed,
As his daughter and Violet held each other and cried.
After giving the matter much consideration,
The king came to terms with this new situation.
All he wanted was for her to be content,
So there was no real reason for him to be bent.

"I love you, Petunia, and I must let you be.
Whatever makes you happy is okay by me!"

It warmed the king's heart, hearing Petunia's laughter,
And the two princesses lived happily ever after.
But the cherry on top of this chocolate-fudge sundae,
Was the king's proclamation, starting this Monday:
"All the peasants below and royals above
Are now free to marry whomever they love."

Art by Mayumi Oda

GIVEN ALL I'VE GOT

Lyrics and music by Jayne Atkinson

Inspired by Jan Tattam

Music on page 147

I've worked so hard to get to this point,
Given all I've got.
But what is the point if what I've got isn't me?

Living a lie and not being free
Is what I've got.
And what is the point if what I've got isn't seen?

I can't live each day, turning my head away,
Because of what people fear, what people will say.
I've got to stand up now, and hold my head up proud,
And be a brighter life for a brighter day.

There's so much I can do,
If I live my life in truth.
Help me throw the lies away—
There's so much I want to say.

Art by Dan Bielefelt

I've worked so hard to get to this point,
Given all I've got.
And what is the point if what I've got isn't seen?

Living in life and living it free
Is what I've got.
And that is the point of living at all—to be me.

I can't live each day, turning my head away,
Because of what people fear, what people will say.
I've got to stand up now, and hold my head up proud,
And be a brighter light for a brighter day.

There's so much I can do,
If I live my life in truth.
I've got to throw the lies away—
There's so much I have to say.

RAPUNZEL

**by Laryssa Husiak with
Barbara June Dodge**

**developed through improvisation
by Fringe Benefits**

This piece is best staged with a lot of action. For example, the NARRATOR should act out the story rather than just narrate it. A no-holds-barred approach is best.

NARRATOR Once upon a time, long, long ago, in the depths of an old forest, there stood an enormous stone castle. Within this castle dwelled a young girl named Rapunzel. *(RAPUNZEL presents herself)* And her bitter, cold Auntie. *(AUNTIE also presents herself)*

(The following sequence is acted out as described—big props!)

Rapunzel's Auntie kept her under very strict lock-and-key up high in her tower. Every day the old Auntie read to Rapunzel from her book—

NARRATOR, AUNTIE and RAPUNZEL *Pretty, Popular and Perfect!*

NARRATOR And made sure she followed *all* the rules.

AUNTIE *(storms into the tower)* Rapunzel! Oh, Rapunzel!!!

RAPUNZEL *(fixing her hair, gazing out the window)* Yes, Auntie.

AUNTIE Oh, what a good girl you are, Rapunzel! It's great to see you fixing your hair. But will you please stop gazing out the window. You know what *Pretty, Popular and Perfect* says: *(displays quote in book)*

AUNTIE and RAPUNZEL "A girl can't ever show a man she is too eager!"

AUNTIE But at least you are taking good care of your hair. Remember, Rappy, your hair is your—

AUNTIE and RAPUNZEL BEST FEATURE!

RAPUNZEL *(obediently)* Yes, Auntie.

AUNTIE Guess what?!!? I dropped by the Clinique counter at Bloomies and brought you some goodies. *(produces a large sack of makeup stuff)*

Art by: (opposite page) Zachary Nicita, PS#1, 6th Grade; (this page, top) Ashley Treacy, Martin Luther King, Jr. Middle School, 6th Grade; (bottom) Flor Juarez, Cragmont School, 4th Grade

RAPUNZEL *(dully)* Thank you, Auntie.

AUNTIE *(stops, sniffs the air)* What do I smell? You haven't been *eating* up here, Rapunzel, have you? Sweetie, what did I say about snacks?

RAPUNZEL But it was only—

AUNTIE If you eat, then you will get FAT. If you get FAT, nobody will like you, then you won't get a husband and that is just the *end*! Goodness, what were you thinking!?

RAPUNZEL I'm so sorry—

AUNTIE And just look at that tushie!! You haven't been doing your "Buns of Steel" exercises, have you!? Tsk … Tsk … Tsk … *(makes Rapunzel do her "Buns of Steel" exercises)* Okay, here we go: and one, and two, and one, and two … Well, I've got to run now, dearie—tanning salon appointment! So, touch up your makeup and let your hair down, so your future husband can see it and climb up to you! And while you're waiting, there's a nifty quiz in *Sweet Teen (hands her the magazine)* that you should work on! Ta-ta, for now!

NARRATOR	So, Rapunzel was left in her tower, alone, waiting for that one special prince to climb up her hair.
RAPUNZEL	*(as she obediently lets down her hair and freshens her makeup)* Ohhh, I do hope someone will come and find me soon! *(pause)* Maybe we could have dinner …

(Singing various superhero and/or adventure movie themes, LIBERTY enters swinging from tree to tree. She discovers RAPUNZEL's hair and swings on it.)

RAPUNZEL	Ouch! Who's down there swinging on my hair?! Gasp! Maybe that's my prince! Excuse me, young man, but what are you doing?

(LIBERTY quickly scurries up RAPUNZEL's hair to her window. RAPUNZEL is shocked to see a girl.)

LIBERTY	Hey!
RAPUNZEL	Hi! Who are you, and what are you doing climbing in those trees and up my hair?
LIBERTY	My name's Liberty and I always climb trees. It's fun! Sorry about your hair … It looked so trippy hanging out the window, I had to see who it belonged to.
RAPUNZEL	You're a girl! You climb well for a girl.
LIBERTY	I climb well, period! *(shows her muscles)*
RAPUNZEL	Wow!
LIBERTY	What're you reading?
RAPUNZEL	*Sweet Teen.* I'm taking the "Am I Perfect Enough for Him?" quiz.
LIBERTY	*(looking it over)* These women look like zombies! Do you really think it's a good idea to let magazines like this tell you how to look and act?
RAPUNZEL	Well, this is what my aunt gets for me to read.
LIBERTY	I bet you sit at this window every day, don't you?
RAPUNZEL	Uh … yes.
LIBERTY	Don't you ever wonder what's out there?
RAPUNZEL	Uh, yes …

LIBERTY	Come out then. *(gets one leg up on the window)* Climb in the trees with me … *(searching for her name)* I didn't even catch your name.
RAPUNZEL	Rapunzel … I don't know if I should—
LIBERTY	What else would you be doing today, Rapunzel?
RAPUNZEL	Well … okay! Can we have a snack?
NARRATOR	Down they went!

(RAPUNZEL and LIBERTY act out the following as the NARRATOR describes it.)

RAPUNZEL and LIBERTY   First floor—Footwear!

(The NARRATOR becomes a tree.)

NARRATOR	Liberty showed Rapunzel how to climb trees and swing from branch to branch! They surprised a nest of baby eagles—

RAPUNZEL and LIBERTY   BOO!

NARRATOR	dodged a swarm of killer bees—

RAPUNZEL and LIBERTY   AAAAHHHH!!!

NARRATOR	but stopped for tea with their queen. *(to girls, offering tea, speaking with a snooty British dialect)* One lump or two?!
RAPUNZEL	*(accepting and sipping tea, also speaking with the dialect)* Lovely weather we're having!
LIBERTY	*(also accepting and sipping tea, and speaking with the dialect)* Charmed, I'm sure!

(All slurp their tea in unison.)

NARRATOR	And they had more fun than you can have in Tarzan's Tree House!

(LIBERTY and RAPUNZEL each do the Tarzan yell.)

NARRATOR	Then all of a sudden Rapunzel's hair got caught in a tree! *(NARRATOR/TREE grabs RAPUNZEL's hair)*
RAPUNZEL	Ouch! OUCH!!!!
LIBERTY	*(quickly turning around)* What's wrong, Rapunzel!?
RAPUNZEL	My hair! It's stuck!! I can't move! Help me!! *(on the verge of tears)*

LIBERTY	Hold on! Just calm down and let me take a look. (*LIBERTY tries to untangle RAPUNZEL's hair but sees there is no hope*) Rapunzel … I hate to tell you this, but your hair is really stuck. I think we're going to have to cut it.

(*AUNTIE enters as if in a flashback or dream sequence.*)

AUNTIE	Oh, Rapunzel! What a good girl. It pleases me to see you fixing your hair. You know, it is your very best feature! Girls would *kill* for hair like that! (*slowly exits, echoing her last words*)
RAPUNZEL	I can't cut my hair!
LIBERTY	Do you want to *stay* stuck!?
RAPUNZEL	But—
LIBERTY	What's the worst that can happen?
RAPUNZEL	Well, without my hair, it's: "Good-bye beauty, good-bye prince, good-bye husband, good-bye happiness!!!"
LIBERTY	Wait a second! How about: "Hello, easy-to-care-for! Hello, I'm me, not my hair! Hello, get out of my way, so that I can climb that tree!!"

(*RAPUNZEL thinks. Then, with a huge smile on her face:*)

RAPUNZEL	You know what? You're right! I don't need my hair for everything, actually, most of the time it just gets in the way! It's like I've been hiding behind my hair

all this time! Gimme those scissors! Good-bye huge tangles! (*cut*) Good-bye split ends! (*cut*) Good-bye hours of shampooing! (*cut*) And most of all: good-bye people who only like me for my hair!! (*cut, cut, cut*)

LIBERTY	Right on!! (*high five*)
RAPUNZEL	Right on!! (*high five*) This is great! I feel so FREEEEEE!!

(*Both girls are very giddy. They dance and spin around.*)

NARRATOR	Rapunzel and Liberty played all afternoon, swinging from tree to tree, running around and having the time of their lives! The sky grew darker and darker, until, finally, it was time for Rapunzel to go home.
RAPUNZEL	I wish this day would never end, Liberty. I've never had so much fun and I've never met a person as wonderful as you. When will we see each other again?
LIBERTY	Don't worry, we'll find each other.
RAPUNZEL	(*à la Dr. Evil, from* Austin Powers: The Spy Who Shagged Me*)* I love you, Mini-Me!
LIBERTY	(*also à la Dr. Evil*) I love you too, Mini-Me!

(*They start to hug.*)

AUNTIE	(*from offstage*) Rapunzel! Oh, Rapunzel!! Have you finished your *Sweet Teen* quiz?!

(*LIBERTY waves good-bye and scrambles down the tower. RAPUNZEL sits innocently. AUNTIE enters RAPUNZEL's room.*)

Oh, excuse me, little boy, I was looking for Rapunzel's tower. Silly me! (*turns around and begins to exit, then stops short*) Wait a second, I only have one tower! (*turns back around*) Rapunzel?! Rapunzel!? AAAAAHHHHH!! (*faints and falls to the ground*)

RAPUNZEL	(*runs to AUNTIE*) Auntie! Auntie! Are you okay!?

AUNTIE   (coming to) Oh! Rapunzel, thank goodness it's you! I thought I just saw you and you had short hair. I'm so glad you have your beautiful, long … (reaches for RAPUNZEL's hair) AAAAAHHHH!! It's true! It *is* you! What have you done?! How could you do this? How? You look so hideous without your hair!! And your mascara is smudged! And your nails!?!? What about femininity, mystery … ?! Who cut this?! I'll SUE!!!

RAPUNZEL   Auntie! Wait … I can explain! I—

AUNTIE   I don't want to hear it! After all that I have done for you, *this* is how you repay me!? You are GROUNDED! You are not leaving this tower until your hair grows back! You'll be up here for a loooong time … MISSY!

(RAPUNZEL stares, shocked, as AUNTIE leaves, locking the door behind her. RAPUNZEL cries.)

RAPUNZEL   I can't take it any longer! She doesn't love me for who I am! She just likes to dress me up like a Barbie doll!!! All my

life I've waited for someone to come and rescue me, but now it's time to rescue myself!

(The following is acted out while spoken.)

NARRATOR   And with that, Rapunzel threw open the window. But, before climbing out, she placed on her bed one lock of her hair with a little Post-it note thanking her Auntie for everything she'd provided for her.

(RAPUNZEL, gives a joyous Tarzan yell as she jumps out the window and runs offstage.)

AUNTIE   (entering) And another thing—

(AUNTIE sees the note and reads it, then grabs the lock of hair, clutches it to her and collapses, weeping hysterically. RAPUNZEL and LIBERTY enter the stage, discover each other, and act out the following as the NARRATOR speaks:)

NARRATOR   Rapunzel swung from tree to tree until she found Liberty once again. They did a little celebration touchdown dance and went off together to explore the world! The End.

Art by Avery Miller, PS#1, 5th Grade

JUST BECAUSE YOU'RE YOU!

by Father Cris Rosales, SDB

Late afternoon, in the kitchen, DAD is reading the newspaper. SON enters slumping, shoulders hunched over, clearly sad.

DAD — Hey, Miguel, how'd the game go today?

SON — *(mumbling, trying not to cry)* Okay, I guess.

DAD — *(looks up from his newspaper, sees SON is upset, puts newspaper down and reaches out to him)* Ay, m'hijo, c'mon, give me a hug. What's wrong?

SON — They were making fun of me in school.

DAD — Why would they do that!?

SON — I dunno … I thought Tommy was my friend, but he made fun of me … He said I was going to hell!

DAD — *¡No seas payaso!* Don't be a clown! Of course you're not going to hell. You're a good boy. Why would you believe that nonsense?

SON — But what if he's right?

DAD — If you're not hurting anybody, you're not going to hell.

SON — How can you be so sure?

DAD — Look at me … *(SON does)* Would I lie to you? *(SON shakes his head no)* I *know*. You're a good boy. They don't take good boys in hell. And don't let anyone tell you otherwise.

SON — What's a *maricon*?

DAD — Is that what they called you? *(SON nods)* Well … *(DAD stands up and sighs)* Maricon is a mean word that some people use to hurt other people's feelings. Sometimes, boys who are brave enough to follow their own path … to not do what all the other boys are doing, whether it's sports or rough-housing or teasing someone … well, these boys sometimes get called *maricon*. It's been going on forever—even way back when I was in school.

SON — Tommy said *maricones* go to hell!

DAD — That was very mean, and he was very wrong!

SON — But—

DAD — Who made you?

SON — God.

DAD — Now why would God create something bad?

SON — He made a mistake?

DAD — God doesn't make mistakes. But people do—like calling each other bad names and not believing that God loves them.

SON — Does God love us all the same?

DAD — Of course! As much as your mom and I love you, that's how much God loves each and every one of his children! God doesn't care whether you can score a touchdown or not, or what grades you get, or how popular you are. God loves you just because you are you!

SON — Wow!

DAD — And do you know why I love you?

SON — Because I'm me?

DAD — *(bear hug)* You got it, *m'hijo.*

Art by Kim Bach 105

THE PARABLE OF THE STIMPLES

by Mark E. Rosenthal

This play may be performed with four, and up to twenty-four (or more), actors. This piece is best staged with a lot of action. For example, the NARRATOR *should act out the story rather than just narrate it. A no-holds-barred approach is best.*

NARRATOR   A long time ago, in a galaxy far, far away …
             There lived a people who were a lot like us.
             They came in all shapes and sizes,
             And colors and smells,
             And walking styles and abilities.
             Some used crutches, some didn't;
             Some spoke with their mouths, some used their hands;
             Some were old, some weren't … yet …
             Some were mothers or fathers, or grandmothers or grandfathers,
                 or uncles or aunts, or cousins–

ALL   AH-HEM!!

NARRATOR   –Or all of these things!
             Now … *some* of these people were born with a special ability: they could make funny noises!

*(*ALL *demonstrate.)*

Art by Hayley Chin, Clover Avenue Elementary, 4th Grade

These people were called—

ALL   THE STIMPLES!

NARRATOR   And making funny noises made them very happy.

ALL   Very, VERY HAPPY!

NARRATOR   Now, there were these other people whom they shared the planet with—

ALL   The BLIMBERS!

NARRATOR   These other folks also came in all shapes, sizes, colors, ages and abilities. Some of them were even related to the Stimples *(or "funny-noise-making-people")*. But, the *big problem* was that everyone was taught that making funny noises was—

BLIMBER #1   BAD!

BLIMBER #2   WRONG!

BLIMBER #3   Something to be afraid of!

NARRATOR   So people were mean to the Stimples.

STIMPLE GIRL   Look what I can do! *(makes a funny noise)*

BLIMBER KID #1   You weirdo!

BLIMBER KID #2   She's a Stimple! She's got COOTIES!!

BLIMBER KID #1 and BLIMBER KID #2 *(pointing at STIMPLE GIRL)*   Nyah, nyah, nyah, nyah, nyah!!

STIMPLE GIRL *(to audience)*   I'm a loser-booger-head!

NARRATOR   Since time began, there have always been Stimples—

(THREE CAVEMEN enter talking "Oooga-Booga." One makes a funny noise. The others hit him with clubs, vocalizing a sound, like: "Wham!" "Whack!" "Boosh!" or "Douge!")

STIMPLE CAVEMAN *(rubbing his head)*   OY!!

NARRATOR   No one knows why the Blimbers didn't like the Stimples.

STIMPLE #1   Why don't they like me?

BLIMBER #4   Because! Now change!

NARRATOR   And some Blimbers really disliked Stimples. They were called—

ALL   MEGMAZOIDS!

NARRATOR   The Megmazoids thought the Stimples were—

MEGMAZOID #1   EVIL!

MEGMAZOID #2   And had to be destroyed!

MEGMAZOID #3   Or changed!

NARRATOR   Which is the same thing to a Stimple. Are you with me so far?
             Now, to be fair, some Blimbers liked Stimples:

BLIMBER #5   I like you!

STIMPLE #2   Thanks!

NARRATOR   And some Blimbers didn't care what noises the Stimples made—as long as they didn't have to hear them:

BLIMBER #6   Make all the noise you want. I just won't listen.

NARRATOR   So, our hero, who happens to be a boy, went to school one day, singing a happy song—

GILBERT   La, la, la …

NARRATOR   Then it happened.

(GILBERT *makes a funny noise, a high-pitched ululation.*)

Now, he liked that noise, so he made it again—

(GILBERT *makes the noise.*)

And again—

(GILBERT *makes the noise.*)

And AGAIN!!!!!!

(GILBERT *makes the noise.*)

He liked it so much that for show-and-tell, he did it AGAIN!

GILBERT   Lookee what I can do! *(makes the funny noise)*

(STUDENTS *gasp!!!*)

TEACHER   GILBERT!!! Go to the principal's office right now!

NARRATOR   See, Gilbert's teacher was a Megmazoid.

TEACHER   Being a Stimple is *bad*!

NARRATOR   Gilbert was confused. What was a Stimple and was he one? And, if so, why was it so bad?

PRINCIPAL   I understand you … uh … made … um … uh … *(cough, cough, etc.)* a noise in class today.

NARRATOR   The principal didn't want to say the "S" word. He thought being a Stimple was something to hide.

PRINCIPAL   *(makes a funny noise and* GILBERT *reacts)* Er … um … excuse me … I mean … Did you hear that? What could that have been?

GILBERT   Well … it sounded like— *(imitates the noise that the* PRINCIPAL *made)*

PRINCIPAL   NEVER MIND! Now, where was I? Oh, yes … Never, ever make that noise again … if you want to keep your job … I mean … if you know what's good for me … I mean you! You know what I mean—people might talk!

GILBERT   Well, what's wrong with that?

PRINCIPAL   Um … I, er … uh … Ask your parents! Do you understand!? *(*GILBERT *nods)*

NARRATOR   Gilbert said yes, even though he didn't.
So, later that night when Gilbert's family was gathered around the dinner table …

MAMA   How was your day, Gilbert?

PAPA   What did you learn in school today, son?

GILBERT   I learned I have a special gift … I can do this:

(GILBERT *makes the funny noise.* MAMA *and* PAPA *fall backward in their chairs.*)

SISTER   Gilbert is a STIMPLE! Gilbert is a STIMPLE!

PAPA   Stop teasing your brother!

MAMA   I won't have name-calling at the dinner table!

PAPA   That's what the living room is for!

GILBERT   What's a Stimple?

MAMA   *(simultaneously with PAPA)* Ask your father!

PAPA   *(simultaneously with MAMA)* Ask your mother!

PAPA and MAMA You're too young to understand.

GILBERT   But why can't I make this noise? *(makes his noise)*

PAPA   Because we said so!

MAMA   Because there are lots of folks out there who don't like STIMPLES.

GILBERT   Why?

MAMA and PAPA We don't know.

MAMA   Just hide that noise—

PAPA   'Cuz we want you to be normal.

MAMA   Like us.

(MAMA and PAPA give GILBERT a great big hug. They freeze, holding forced smiles.)

NARRATOR   So, Gilbert didn't make that noise in public anymore,
               'Cuz he loved his parents and didn't want to upset them.
               And time went by,
               And Gilbert got bigger,
               And he almost forgot about his talent …
               'Til one day …

STUDENT #1   OMIGOSH! Did you hear about Ms. Flimmer-Flammer?

STUDENT #2   No, what!?

STUDENT #1   I heard … she got caught making a NOISE!

(STUDENT #1 and STUDENT #2 scream and giggle.)

GILBERT   Not her?!

STUDENT #1   Yes, her! Can you believe it!?

STUDENT #2   I always knew she was a STIMPLE!!

STUDENT #1   Eeeew!! Gross!

STUDENT #2   I know! What a FREAK!

STUDENT #1 and STUDENT #2   She makes me SICK!

GILBERT   *(simply)* Just because she's a Stimple doesn't mean she's a bad person.

STUDENT #1 and STUDENT #2   Yes it does!

GILBERT   Why?

STUDENT #1   I'm sure!

STUDENT #2   Do you have to ask?

GILBERT   Well, I like her!

STUDENT #2   You would!

STUDENT #1   I always thought you were weird!

STUDENT #2   Why don't you just move to STIMPLEVILLE with her!?

STUDENT #1   Yeah, 'cuz she's not gonna teach here anymore—she's getting fired!

(STUDENT #1 and STUDENT #2 give each other a high five and exit laughing.)

GILBERT   (to audience) Fired? For being a Stimple?

NARRATOR   Gilbert thought he'd see if there was anything he could do to help Ms. Flimmer-Flammer.

GILBERT   Ms. Flimmer-Flammer?!

MS. FLIMMER-FLAMMER   Hello, Gilbert.

GILBERT   I heard what happened. I'm sorry. Is it true? ... Are you really a ... ?!

MS. FLIMMER-FLAMMER   Why, yes, I am, Gilbert. I'm glad I can say it now. I am a Stimple.
Does that bother you?

GILBERT   No, not at all. You're still the same person. Of course I still like you.

MS. FLIMMER-FLAMMER   Thank you, Gilbert. That means a lot to me. I wish everyone felt that way.

GILBERT   It makes me sad to think that people judge us for the noises we make.

MS. FLIMMER-FLAMMER   Maybe some day they'll understand.

(The CROWD enters from offstage, repeating the following three times:)

CROWD   DOWN WITH STIMPLES! NO MORE STIMPLES!

GILBERT   What's going on!?

(GILBERT runs "outside" to see what's happening. The actor playing MS. FLIMMER-FLAMMER quickly slips out of character to join the CROWD—angry people, who yell and carry picket signs such as: SILENCE = NORMAL, STIMPLES STINK!, DON'T MAKE A NOISE!, KEEP QUIET!, FIRE FLIMMER-FLAMMER! and DOWN WITH STIMPLES!, etc. The CROWD's lines may be divided up, some spoken in unison, others spoken by individual CROWD members, etc.)

CROWD   STIMPLES stink! They're not like us!
We should put them on a bus!
Fire Flimmer-Flammer! She's a creep!
Our school needs an ANTI-STIMPLE sweep!!
Fire the STIMPLES! Burn the books!
And while you're at it, fire the BIZNOOKS!!
Get rid of the CLINKLEFRATS, they won't do!
And the QUARKMIMNOIDS and the ZYBLEROO!
We know what's best, as you all can see!
Now we have spoken, and SO IT SHALL BE!!!

GILBERT   (overlapping his "BE" with the CROWD's "BE") BE QUIET!!!!!!

(The CROWD shuts up.)

MEGMAZOID #1   (laughs) You can't make us!

MEGMAZOID #2   (taunting) Nyah, nyah, nyah!!!

MEGMAZOID #3   Why do you care, anyways?!

GILBERT   Ms. Flimmer-Flammer is my favorite teacher and being a Stimple doesn't make her bad!

CROWD   (closing in on GILBERT) Any friend of theirs is no friend of ours!

GILBERT   You're no better than us—

(Everyone gasps!!!!!)

I mean them.

MEGMAZOID #1   You're one of them, aren't you?!

MEGMAZOID #2   You're sick!

MEGMAZOID #3   Disgusting!

GILBERT   No, I'm not!

MEGMAZOID #2   You can *change*!

MEGMAZOID #1   You *have* to change!

MEGMAZOID #3   *Otherwise*, we won't like you!

GILBERT   You don't like anybody who isn't exactly like you!

CROWD   LET'S GET HIM!!

(The CROWD jumps GILBERT.)

NARRATOR   Freeze!!

(The CROWD freezes on the brink of violence.)

              Just then, Gilbert discovered something verrrrrrry interesting—

(GILBERT makes his noise again and the CROWD gasps and shrinks back!)

NARRATOR   The MEGMAZOIDS were *afraid* of the funny noises!
              Quick! Quick, everybody, we need your help!
              Help save Gilbert and
              ALL of the STIMPLES in the world,
              Who get yelled at and bullied by the MEGMAZOIDS!!
              Quick! Make a noise! Quick! Quick!

(Hopefully the audience makes a lot of noises, encouraged by the NARRATOR and GILBERT, and the CROWD of Megmazoids withers, screams and runs away.)

GILBERT   Thank you … *(out of breath)* You saved my life—All of you!!

NARRATOR   Well, you're half right. We helped you … But we couldn't have done it without you!

GILBERT   WE BEAT 'EM!!

NARRATOR   They'll be back!

MEGMAZOID #1   *(pops on)* We'll be back!!

NARRATOR   We haven't heard the last of them!

MEGMAZOID #2   *(pops on)* Hey!! That's my line!! You haven't heard the last of us!

NARRATOR   Oh, really!? *(makes a funny noise and chases MEGMAZOID #2 offstage)*

GILBERT   I just don't understand why everyone's so afraid of our funny noises! *(pauses to think—light bulb!!!)*
              Hey … Hey … What if … We all got together … all of us Stimples, and we *stopped hiding* our
              talent—

NARRATOR   Learned to be *proud*—

GILBERT   Proud of what makes us each special! Then everyone would see that we're nothing to be afraid of!!!

(During the following, BLIMBERS and STIMPLES reenter with parade paraphernalia, for example: balloons, colorful placards and banners; MAMA and PAPA with a rainbow banner: BLIMBERS ♥ STIMPLES; and others with signs saying: EXPRESS YOURSELF! DIFFERENT IS GREAT! etc. Divide up the NARRATOR's lines among the characters already seen, as seems most appropriate.)

NARRATOR So, Gilbert set out to gather all the Stimples together.
And his mom and dad, even though they were Blimbers, they helped, too!
They searched the land and they searched the sea,
And suddenly it seemed like there were more Stimples than ever before!
Young ones! Old ones! Shy ones! Bold ones!
Doctors, teachers, parents, too—from Quinkleyburg to Halaroo!

GILBERT And lots of Blimbers stopped being afraid,
When the Stimples all gathered and had a parade! *(tosses confetti)*

NARRATOR The Blimbers saw Stimples were just like them:
Some were even their parents and friends!
They weren't all monsters or creatures or freaks!
They even saw some on TV every week!
So, once the Blimbers saw there was nothing to fear,
Then those "weird," "funky" Stimples didn't seem quite so "queer."
They laughed at the same things! They didn't have warts!
Some were very religious. Some even played sports!
But, the one thing in common all these folks did share,
Wasn't their thoughts or the clothes they would wear:
It's that they were all *human*, with blood in their veins,
And snot in their noses, and thoughts in their brains!
When you line us all up, all the Blimbers and Stimples,
All the Megmazoids, Dunkleborgs, Weee-Wahs and Zimples,
Can you tell who we are by the way that we look?!
Or the games that we play?! Or the food that we cook?!
It's hard enough really to know who *you* are,
And with other people, it's much harder by far!
Stimples are *ev'rywhere*, so watch what you say!
And don't tease the people you think are "that way,"
'Cuz we all were sitting where you are today!
And you might know, love or *be* a Stimple some day!

WE CAN CHANGE

THE WORLD!

Ari Morcos, 9

"My rabbi walked hand-in-hand with Martin Luther King, Jr., on the Peace Walk. I think that rocks!"

WE CAN CHANGE THE WORLD!

Foundations School Community, Woodland Hills, Lynn Capri's 4th and 5th Grade Leaders

Baylee Connor Deanna

Melissa

Ms. Capri

Ari A.J. Jon Ariane

Deanna Herbert, 11

"I think that everyone should stand up for what they believe in, just like Martin Luther King."

Ariane Lange, 10

"I would like everybody to be treated equally, whether they are popular, unpopular, short, tall, different, smart, not getting good grades, getting good grades, believing in things, not believing in things, ugly, pretty, cool, not so cool, glasses, braces, rich, poor or in between."

Photo by Joanne Lange

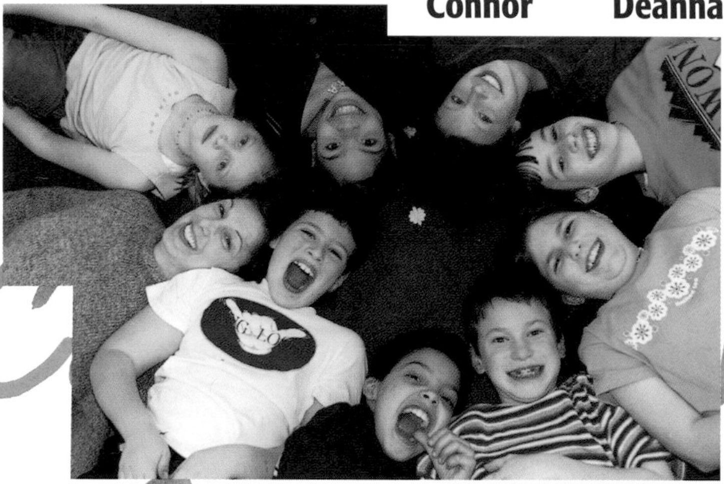

MELISSA COBER, 11

"I think it is important to study historic people because you can learn good lessons from them."

A. J. ERICKSON, 11

"I want to change the world."

CONNOR KELLY-EIDING, 11

"If there's someone who's being pushed around, you should be brave, like Harriet Tubman, and go up to the person who's being pushed around and help him or her."

JON E. BROWN, 11

"I still think girls are the ones with cooties."

Ariane Lange

Deanna Herbert

BAYLEE DOVALL, 11

"It feels awful to know that people have not changed their ideas about other races."

115

RIPPLE EFFECT

by Mark E. Rosenthal

Someday, I'll be able to:
Be who I am
Wear what I want
Go where I choose
Get what I need
Grow new ideas
Shine like the sun
See I belong
Be unafraid
Feel proud of me
Share all I am
Change my whole world
Love without fear
Be safe from hate
Become Ms. President!

Imagine a place where there is:
No reason to hide
No teasing, no loneliness
No yelling, no growling
No pushing, no shoving
No screaming, no hatred
No gangs, no countries
One people, one world!

That place is here.

Someday is today.

"Each time a man stands up for an ideal
Or acts to improve the lot of others
Or strikes out against injustice,
He sends forth a tiny ripple of hope.
And crossing each other from a million
Different centers of energy and daring,
Those ripples build a current that can
Sweep down the mightiest walls of
Oppression and resistance."

–*Robert Kennedy, 1966*

That time is now.

Your thoughts, your words, your deeds …
In all of history, there has been and will only be
ONE YOU!
If you don't speak up,
Your voice will never be heard.

That person is me.

LIBERTY!

Excerpted from *Liberty!*, a one-man show by Chris Wells

There should be an introduction that says something simple, such as: "Ladies and gentlemen, it is our pleasure to welcome to (*fill in the blank*) School, the Statue of Liberty!

The STATUE OF LIBERTY should be revealed standing in the classic pose. After several beats, she smiles warmly at the audience, but then resumes her pose. This is repeated until she can no longer contain her joy at being with these kids at this school. Then she breaks her pose to speak. If this gradual coming-to-life is not possible, the STATUE OF LIBERTY should enter from the back of the house or another less traditional entrance.

LIBERTY   Bonjour! Salut. Ça va? Je suis tellement heureuse de voir tant des beaux visages devant moi!! O, je m'excuse, vous ne comprenez pas le Français.

My name is Liberty. My full name is Liberty Enlightening zee World. I am so happy to be here at (*insert name of school*) wiss all of you. I am loving America very much.

Oh beautiful for spacious skies ... God bless America, sroo zee night wiss a light from above ... Ziss land is your land ... ziss land is my land ... Sweet land of liberty ... I love zee lonely highways, zee beautiful state parks, zee Walmart, zee children playing in zee front yards ...

And,
now, ere I
am wiss all of you!
At (*insert name of school*)!
Ziss is what I love. In America, we have options, always zee options.
Zee option to move, par example!
I'm going on a trip and I'm taking an (A) audience.
I'm going on a trip and I'm taking an (A) audience and a (B) book.
I'm going on a trip and I'm taking an (A) audience and a (B) book and
a (C) crown
And (D) Declaration of Independence
And (E) equality and (F) freedom
And (G) give me your tired, your poor, your (H) huddled masses
   yearning to breathe free.
Your (I) Independence and right to a (J) jury trial
(K) keep ancient lands your story pomp
(L) love it or leave it
(M) the Mississippi River, (N) Niagara Falls
(OOOOOO) Oklahoma
(P) peace, the prairies and Pocahontas
(Q) question authority
(R) Rights, as in the Bill of
(S) send these, the homeless tempest
   tossed (T) to me
(U) under, as in: "One nation under God"
(V) is for Victory—my sister!
   "We the People"
Xerox, Xerox, Xerox Corporation
Y is for yes, yes, yes, yes—the best word
   in America
And (Z) is for ziss, as in ziss is my
   country!!

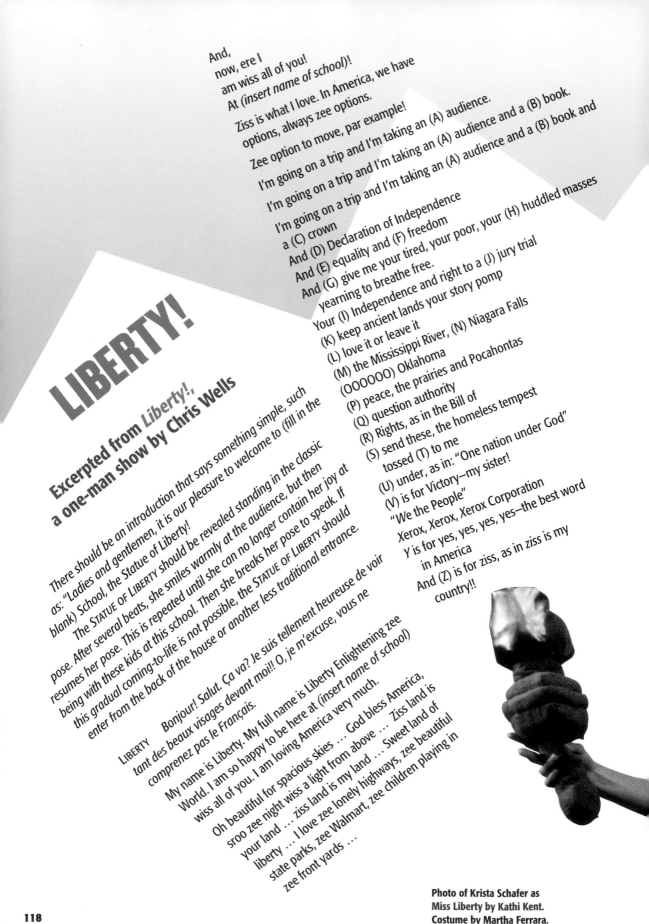

Photo of Krista Schafer as Miss Liberty by Kathi Kent. Costume by Martha Ferrara.

(She sits, exhausted.)

I only have one day off and I must get back to my island, but I have so much to do … I am studying for the test for American citizenship. Will you help me? *(encourages kids to respond)*

July Fourth is our Independence Day … Independence from whom? Independence from whom? *(encourages kids to respond)* England, that's right!

What does zee Declaration of Independence say? *(remembers)* All men, women and babies are created equal. Absolutely everybody is created equal, whether they're Asian, Latino, African, Caucasian, Native American, Catholic, Buddhist, Muslim, Jewish, Christian, gay, straight, rich, poor, blind or sighted, German, Arab, Polish, postal workers, presidents or *poodle trainers* or all of the above!

Why did the pilgrims come to America? To get to the other side? No … freedom.

And now, the Bill of Rights: freedom of speech, freedom of the press. Can you change the system? *(encourages kids to respond)* You can request it, yes.

So many questions to become an American … So many things to remember. But what I never forget is: zee poem zat was written for me when I was born. I'll tell you a little bit:

Give me your tired, your poor,
Your huddled masses yearning to breathe free,
Zee wretched refuse of your teeming shore.
Send zees, zee homeless, tempest tossed to me.
I lift my lamp beside zee golden door!!

I love ziss poem! It reminds me what my job is: To welcome you all to the land of the free, where even a 150-foot-tall, green French woman can get a job!

Omymy … LOOK AT ZEEE TIME!!! Oh, I must go, I 'ave to get back to work. Good-bye, everyone! Sank you! Au revoir!!
(She exits.)

FOUR HEROES
by Peter Howard

DARRYL *enters carrying an assortment of objects: a boombox, a handful of colored streamers or confetti, a rolled-up poster, an easel. He hums "Happy Birthday" as he arranges the objects and sets up the easel, which displays a large calendar. He sticks a big gold star on today's date on the calendar.*

He reaches down and turns on the boombox. Loud music of a marching band and the sound of a screaming crowd is heard. DARRYL *begins a wild little solo celebration. He dances, waves and throws kisses to the crowd. He throws the streamers in the air, accepts the applause of the grateful "crowd." He is enormously touched and overwhelmed.*

At some point during this celebration, ANDY *enters.* DARRYL *notices* ANDY *and tries to involve him in the celebration, but* ANDY *resists.*

Art by Suk Gyu Sean Kim, Clover Avenue Elementary, 4th Grade

Photos are courtesy of Corbis: Susan B. Anthony (p. 122); Cesar Chavez (p. 123); Rosa Parks (p. 124); Harvey Milk (p. 125)

120

ANDY   You okay?

DARRYL   Happy Darryl Day!

ANDY   Darryl …

DARRYL   Close all the schools! Close all the stores! Start the parade! It's Darryl Day! *(insert today's date)* is a national holiday!

*(*ANDY *turns off the music.)*

ANDY   There's no such thing as Darryl Day.

DARRYL   There will be. We celebrate birthdays, right? With parties and stuff? And when someone is really special, we make their birthday a holiday, right? Like Martin Luther King, Jr., Day, or Presidents Day.

ANDY   But you're just … Darryl.

DARRYL   I'm special enough. Darryl Day will be the happiest day of the year. Everyone will have the day off from work or school. And everyone in the country will give me presents. *(unrolls a poster—a drawing, photo or cartoon—bearing his likeness, which proclaims the new holiday)*

ANDY   Those holidays—like Martin Luther King, Jr., Day—they're not about getting presents. They're not about *getting* anything. They're about *giving*.

DARRYL   Giving? Giving what?

ANDY   Dr. Martin Luther King, Jr., gave us hope, and he gave us the courage to work for equal rights. That's why we celebrate his birthday.

DARRYL   Well, I give things, too. Yesterday, I gave you my pizza crust.

*(*BETH *enters; she watches and listens.)*

ANDY   Now, I'll tell you what should be a holiday: February 15th— *(changes the calendar to February and sticks the star on the 15th)* Susan B. Anthony's birthday.

BETH   Susan B. Anthony? The suffragist? She was amazing.

DARRYL Suffragist? What's that?

BETH   Someone who worked for the right to vote. Not that long ago women weren't allowed to vote in this country.

ANDY   (as he pulls out his favorite image of Susan B. Anthony: a poster, line drawing, cartoon, book jacket, etc.) She was born on February 15, 1820. She lived in a time when women couldn't go to college and they could only have the lowest paying jobs—

BETH   Like working in sweatshops for fourteen hours a day!

ANDY   She spent her whole life trying to help everyone—black and white, male and female—get a voice and a vote in this country.

DARRYL So, how would we celebrate Susan B. Anthony Day? With a parade?

BETH   Nope. I know. Wait a second. (disappears for a moment, and returns with a pair of bloomers. She pulls them on while she speaks) On Susan B. Anthony Day, everybody wears bloomers.

(DARRYL erupts in laughter when seeing the bloomers.)

        That's exactly what happened to Susan. Everybody laughed at her.

ANDY   Back then, women's clothes were uncomfortable. They had to wear corsets and stiff skirts. It was hard to move and breathe.

BETH   Susan and her suffragist friends—

ANDY   Like Amelia Bloomer—

BETH   wanted to change things. They wore the first pants for women, and called them bloomers.

ANDY   And people laughed. They insulted her and threatened her. But she kept going. On the day she died she said, "The fight must not cease; you must see that it does not stop. Failure is impossible."

BETH   And in 1920, a hundred years after she was born, Susan B. Anthony's dream came true. The women of America voted for the very first time.

(LISA enters, snacking on an apple.)

LISA   (to BETH) Nice pajamas.

DARRYL They're bloomers. We're practicing for Susan B. Anthony Day.

LISA   February 15th, right? Good choice. She's cool. And how about— (changing the calendar) March 31st?

ANDY   Why?

LISA   That's the day Cesar Chavez was born in 1927! (pulls out an image of Cesar Chavez and hands it to BETH, who unrolls it)

DARRYL Who's he?

LISA   Well, see this apple? *(starts to cut it and offers slices to everyone)* Somebody had to pick it, right? Just like someone picks every fruit and vegetable that we eat. Cesar fought for the rights of those people. See, when he was a boy in Arizona, he worked as a migrant farm worker, moving around a lot, picking crops under the hot sun for low wages. His family moved so often, he went to more than thirty different elementary schools.

DARRYL   Whoa.

LISA   When he grew up, he helped start a union— the United Farm Workers. He led peaceful protests, like *La Huelga*—

BETH   The strike—

LISA   against the big grape growers. He was a leader of *La Raza*.

ANDY   The Mexican-American people.

LISA   Cesar fought for the rights of all people— African-Americans, women and, in his later years, for gays and lesbians. He once said, "It is my deepest belief that only by giving our lives do we find life."

DARRYL   There's that giving thing again.

BETH   Hey, I've got another one. *(changing the calendar)* February 4th. Any guesses?

DARRYL   Give us a hint.

BETH   It's a woman …

DARRYL   Give us another hint.

BETH   She was very brave … She wouldn't give up her seat … Anyone else want to guess?

(BETH turns to the audience and takes guesses from them. If someone gets it, terrific. If not, no problem. Either way, she pulls out and displays her Rosa Parks image.)

    Yes! Rosa Parks. Born in Alabama on February 4, 1913. She grew up in the segregated South.

LISA   That was when black people and white people had to go to separate schools—

DARRYL   And drink from separate water fountains—

BETH   And ride in different parts of the bus. Black people had to sit in the back.

ANDY   I like the back—you get the bounciest ride!

DARRYL   Maybe so, but you get to choose.

(The group enacts the bus incident through simple mime as BETH tells the story.)

BETH   Everybody gets to choose now, thanks to Rosa Parks and the NAACP. It all started one cold December afternoon in 1955. Rosa paid her fare and took a seat. And along came a white man who told her—

DARRYL   "Let me have that seat."

BETH   But Rosa didn't move. Rosa wasn't tired; she was just tired of giving in.

ANDY   What happened next?

BETH   She got arrested. But Rosa and her husband and a group of local ministers—

DARRYL   Including Martin Luther King, Jr.—

LISA   Had a plan. Since the bus system was unfair to black people, black people would boycott the buses and walk.

DARRYL   And did they ever walk! They walked to work and home again for a whole year. The streets were full of proud African-American people, walking.

LISA   The bus company lost money and had to change its rules.

BETH   And Rosa Parks became known as "The Mother of the Civil Rights Movement," inspiring people all over the world to stand up—

DARRYL   Or sit down—

BETH   Or sit down for what's right.

DARRYL   I think I get it!

BETH   Get what?

DARRYL   This whole holiday thing. I know another birthday we should celebrate.

ANDY, BETH and LISA   Darryl Day?!

DARRYL   No, not Darryl Day. Give me one second. *(runs offstage and returns with a rolled-up poster of his own)* I get it now. We should celebrate the givers—people who give of themselves to make the world better for others. People like Susan B. Anthony, who never give up, even when they're laughed at. People like Cesar Chavez, who are peaceful and caring. People like Rosa Parks, who are brave in the face of danger. People like— *(takes a suspenseful pause)* Drum roll please *(someone imitates a drum roll)* —Harvey Milk! *(DARRYL presents his favorite image of Harvey Milk)*

124

ANDY and BETH   Harvey Milk?

DARRYL   *(changing the calendar)* Harvey Milk Day! May 22nd! Harvey was born on May 22, 1930!

BETH   Who's Harvey Milk?

DARRYL   He was the first openly gay person to win an election in the United States.

LISA   My grandpa said he was a great guy. They called him "The Mayor of Castro Street," right?

DARRYL   Yep. And as a District Supervisor in San Francisco, he worked hard for better schools, for clean city streets, for senior citizens. He worked hard to defeat a plan that would have caused teachers to lose their jobs just because they were gay or lesbian.

BETH   You mean, if it weren't for him, we couldn't have Mr. Navarro for band?

LISA   Or Ms. Olson for fifth grade!

BETH   Wow.

DARRYL   When Harvey Milk got elected, he said, "If a gay man can win, it proves that there is hope for all minorities who are willing to fight."

LISA   He brought people together and gave them hope.

DARRYL   On the day he died, thousands of people—gay and straight, from all over San Francisco—joined together, carrying candles and marching to the beat of a single, steady drum. *(imitates a drum, and marches in place for a moment or two)*

LISA   *(joining the "march")* In San Francisco, they celebrate Harvey Milk Day and reenact that march every year. Grandpa took me. It was really beautiful.

(Pause.)

BETH   You know, someone once asked Rosa Parks if she liked the idea of a Rosa Parks Day.

ANDY   What did she say?

BETH   She said, "I would rather our world reach a point where every day is a day of honor for everyone. We would not need national days of recognition if everyone in our society were recognized for what they are: children of God with the potential to make a great contribution to our world."

ANDY   You were right all along, Darryl.

DARRYL   I was?

ANDY   Every day should be Darryl Day!

LISA   And Andy Day!

BETH   And Lisa Day!

DARRYL   And Beth Day! Happy Darryl Day, everyone!

(Someone turns on the boombox. The cast dances and throws confetti.)

   You know, you can still give me presents if you want to!

ANDY, BETH and LISA   Darryl!

(They chase DARRYL offstage.)

Art by Ned Bittinger

SHY KEVIN
AND CURIOUS JOE

by Joseph Brouillette

A school yard. The lunch bell rings. Children enter from the wings and fill the stage. They cause general commotion—laughing, running, pinching and poking each other. They form groups and settle in, passing their lunch time on stage. One boy, KEVIN, sits all alone. He starts to unpack his lunch. Another boy, JOE, enters with his lunch bag. He notices KEVIN and comes up behind him.

JOE   Hi!

(No response from KEVIN.)

          Hi!

(Still no response.)

          I said, "Hi!" What are you, deaf?!

(JOE approaches KEVIN and sits next to him.)

KEVIN   *(looks up and waves)* Hi.

JOE   Well, now you say hi. Jeez, I was calling from back there.

KEVIN   *(with a speech impediment)* I did not hear you.

JOE   Why not?

KEVIN   I'm deaf.

JOE   Ah, stop foolin'.

KEVIN   No, really.

JOE   Really?

KEVIN   Yeah.

JOE   *(pulls a sandwich out of his lunch bag)* So, how do you know what I'm saying?

KEVIN	I can read your lips.
JOE	No foolin'?
KEVIN	I really can.
JOE	*(covers his mouth)* My dog has fleas. *(uncovers his mouth)* What did I say?
KEVIN	I don't know.
JOE	You're really deaf, then. Wow.
KEVIN	Yeah. Look. *(points to his hearing aid)*
JOE	What's that thing?
KEVIN	My hearing aid.
JOE	What does it do?
KEVIN	It helps me hear.
JOE	But I thought you couldn't hear.
KEVIN	It helps me hear high and loud things, like sirens.
JOE	Like this? *(imitates the noise an ambulance makes)*
KEVIN	*(winces)* Yeah, like that.
JOE	What about this? *(whispering)* My dog has fleas.
KEVIN	Your dog has fleas?
JOE	You heard that?
KEVIN	No. I read your lips.
JOE	*(smiles)* What's your name?
KEVIN	*(signs his name and says it at the same time)* Kevin.
JOE	Is that your sign language name?
KEVIN	Yep.
JOE	I'm Joe. What's my sign language name?
KEVIN	Everyone has their own.
JOE	How come?
KEVIN	Because your name fits your personality.
JOE	What does your name mean?
KEVIN	It means "Shy Kevin."

JOE	So give me a name.

(KEVIN signs a "J" on the chin.)

	What does that mean?
KEVIN	It means "Curious Joe."
JOE	I'm curious?
KEVIN	Yes, you are.
JOE	Why are you shy?
KEVIN	I dunno. Just am.
JOE	Are you afraid?
KEVIN	Afraid of what?
JOE	Afraid of people?
KEVIN	Maybe. I don't like it when they make fun of me.
JOE	Why would they do that?
KEVIN	They say I talk funny. *(sees two BULLIES coming toward them)* Uh-oh.
BULLY #1	Look, it's the dumb-dumb who can't talk.
BULLY #2	And his dumb-dumb friend. *(imitating KEVIN's impediment)* I can't talk right because I'm so stupid.
JOE	He is not stupid. Leave him alone.
BULLY #1	He is too. He's so dumb, he has to talk with his hands, like a monkey.

(The two laugh meanly and walk away.)

JOE	Don't listen to them. I think you're smart. Smarter than both of them put together.
KEVIN	You think?
JOE	I know. How do you say "smart?"

(KEVIN points to his forehead. JOE signs: "Kevin–smart.")

KEVIN	*(smiles and signs: "Joe–nice–friend")* Joe, nice friend.
JOE	What did you say?
KEVIN	I said, "Joe is a nice friend."
JOE	*(sticks out his hand with his index finger extended, just like KEVIN)* Friends?
KEVIN	Friends.

(KEVIN connects his index finger with JOE's, making the sign for "friends." They address the audience. When one speaks, the other signs.)

JOE   That was us in third grade. Kevin and I have been friends now for many, many years. Over those years, we've learned a lot about each other's culture, and even some history. In fact, there have been quite a few very smart, very capable, deaf people in history. Just to give a few examples: Erastus Smith was a soldier and spy who was able to get important secrets by reading the enemy's lips. And Ludwig van Beethoven, the famous composer, he went deaf at age thirty but continued to write beautiful music even though he could hear it only in his mind!! Thomas Edison, inventor of the light bulb, record player and many other ingenious devices, went deaf when he was only twelve years old. And there's Marlee Matlin, a deaf actress, who has been in Broadway plays, Hollywood movies and TV shows. She even won an Academy Award!

KEVIN   Don't forget Helen Keller!

JOE   Yeah! Helen Keller was deaf and blind, which meant she couldn't hear or see anything. But she learned to communicate by using her hands and her sense of touch, and she taught many other deaf-blind people to do the same.

KEVIN   Deaf people, just like the hearing, can accomplish anything we put our minds to. Just because we have a different language and wear hearing aids doesn't make us any less smart, less funny, less normal, less anything. And it certainly doesn't mean we can't be your friend. You want to be a friend? Just put your fingers together like this, and then flip them over. That makes you a friend. *(both KEVIN and JOE show the audience how to make the sign for "friend" and then encourage them to make it, too)* Try it again. Good. Now you're all friends!

JOE   One last thing. To clap your hands as the deaf do and show your appreciation, instead of putting them together and making all that noise, just raise them in the air and wave.

(Both demonstrate and encourage the audience to follow.)

KEVIN and JOE   Hooray! Good job!

(They bow as the applause continues.)

BILLY TIPTON

Excerpted from *The Opposite Sex Is Neither* by Kate Bornstein

Sounds of a Billy Tipton piano recording.

BILLY   I'm here! I'm really here! All right. All right. Oh! 'scuse me. Name's Billy. How do? See, I died a few years ago, and I been watchin' ever since.

So for all this time—for these long years—I've been the chill that goes up your spine when you hear good jazz. That's right! I've been the ghost of Swing. The poltergeist in your parlor piano. Solid Jackson! Good to be back on a stage again. Righteous! No piano, though. Don't that just figure? But hey—dig this: *(snaps his fingers, and his piano music starts to play)* lots you can do, lots you can do this side of life.

But listen to me. Please. From what I figured out, that's what you're supposed to do. All I wanted to do was blow my horn, tickle my ivories, make some music. Dang! The girls came 'round when I made my music. Solid, Jackson! I don't make music anymore. All that talk about music in heaven? Forget it. I sold my piano before I died, and they buried me without my horn.

But, dig it—have you ever wanted something so bad it made you crazy not to have it. Man, that was my music, do you dig? I had this music playing in my head. But they said to me: "Honey, Swing is for men." *"Honey"!*

Oh, I could've been a girl singer with one of the bands, but I didn't want that. I didn't want that treatment. And the music, it built up in my head. I tried acting like a woman was "supposed to." I did! I even wore a dress. Once.

I found this one club where the band was all old men. I'd sneak down there, and they let me play my horn—behind the curtain. Man's gotta do what a man's gotta do. I couldn't sleep. I wouldn't eat. I was delirious happy. Can you dig it? There's just nothing I want to be closer to than my music. And I knew that back then.

One night, after a year of playin' behind that curtain, I went down to the club and it was closed up. I never found out what happened to it. I never saw the old men again. I went crazy nuts. I woke up in an alley, with these kids kickin' me. And they were sayin', "Mister, hey, mister." And I thought to myself, Mister? Mister? And then I thought, Yeah, why not "mister." And right then, right then I knew what I would do. And I was Billy from that moment on. Felt right. Lord, it felt right. For the first time in my life, it felt so very right.

SAME WORLD

Lyrics and music by Jayne Atkinson and Katherine Reclusado

Music on page 149

I walked as a child
To the top of the hill,
I tried to find the sun.
The world seemed so big,
So what could I give,
When I feel I don't fit in?

And the mystery unfurls:
I am caught between, caught between two worlds.

In the middle I stand,
I am who I am:
There's no right or wrong.
So I've made my choice—
Please hear my voice—
I have found where I belong.

'Cuz I've seen the mystery unfurl:
I've been caught between, caught between two worlds.

I'm a spirit from God.
I'm a person of love.
I can no longer be in disguise.
I've come out of the dark,
Learning to open my heart.
Touch me and I'll touch you:
You will see we come from the same world.

I walked as a child
To the top of the hill.
With all my faith I can believe:
I can hold my head high, carry truth in my eyes;
I have finally found my peace.

The sacred mystery unfurls:
We are all from, all from the same world!
We are all from the same world!

WHAT'S WITH THE DRESS, JACK?

**by Amity Westcott
with Erik R. Stegman**

Dedicated to Jésus and Yubiani

*JILL, ten, is playing with toy trucks in
JACK'S living room.*

JILL   *(calling offstage to her friend, JACK)*
         C'mon, Jack, I'm not doing the Crash-
         Up Derby without you!

JACK   Just a second!

JILL   I don't think your auntie is going to like
         it if she finds you messin' around in her
         room.

(JACK, ten, enters.)

JACK   Ta-da!

JILL   What's with the dress, Jack?

JACK   Do you like it? I picked it out myself.

JILL   It's … um … flowery.

JACK   It shows off my legs.

JILL   Yeah, Jack, your *hairy* legs!

JACK   I just thought I'd try something
         different, something pretty. I get kind of
         tired of wearing jeans and T-shirts all
         the time.

We'wha in the ceremonial costume of Zuni women.

JILL	But, Jack, boys don't wear dresses.
JACK	This boy does!
JILL	Okay, first it was your grandma's clip-on earrings, then it was glitter body gel, and last week you wore my butterfly clips to *school* … now a DRESS?! You goin' crazy on me?
JACK	I'm not crazy. We had a speaker come to school today, this really famous weaver from the Assiniboine tribe of the Sioux Nation. His name's Running Eagle and he wore a beautiful dress he'd made himself!
JILL	What!? He wore a DRESS?! Men don't wear dresses! And American Indian men *definitely* don't wear dresses–they're all chiefs or warriors or hunters!
JACK	That's what I thought, too. But a lot of American Indian tribes believe that your SPIRIT, not your body, tells you what to wear and what to do.
JILL	*Our spirit?* You mean, like what's inside of us?
JACK	Yeah … like when Running Eagle was little, he played with dolls and liked basket-weaving, and he felt like he was a girl. And since that's how he felt and how he wanted to be, that's what he—or, I guess, she—did!
JILL	I don't get it … is this Running Eagle person a man or a woman?!
JACK	Well, both, kinda. Since Running Eagle has the body of a man but the spirit of a woman, she's what the American Indians call a "two-spirit."
JILL	A two-spirit?
JACK	Yeah, like half-boy, half-girl … Two spirits.
JILL	I bet she got teased *a lot* growing up!
JACK	Nope! Her mom and dad and everyone in her tribe were totally cool with it. In fact, there are American Indians all over the country from all different tribes who are *official* two-spirits. And their tribes really, really respect them, no matter how they dress or what kinda work they wanna do!
JILL	It's different where we live.
JACK	It doesn't have to be.

(Pause.)

JILL	Maybe not … My uncle's a nurse. That used to be considered "women's work."
JACK	Yeah … and y'know Ms. Ramirez down the street … the one who builds houses and has that *really* cool tool belt?
JILL	*(laughs)* Yeah. My dad is so jealous of that belt!
JACK	Most people think of men building houses not women, but she does it anyway!
JILL	Yeah!
JACK	And did you ever notice that girls wear boys' clothes all the time, and it's, like, no biggie.
JILL	Like my sister: she's *always* borrowing her boyfriend's shirts, and no one makes fun of her!
JACK	Mmm-hmm! So, why can't boys wear girls' clothes?!
JILL	Well …
JACK	Well, what?
JILL	Well, I guess that's only fair, but–
JACK	Yes …
JILL	You might wanna wear something a little more fashionable! I'm sorry, Jack, but flowery is out! It's all about solid colors!
JACK	It is?
JILL	*(laughs)* Oh, Jack, you still have a lot to learn! Hey, let's go back to my house and I'll give you a makeover!
JACK	Excellent! And then we can have the Crash-Up Derby in your backyard!

MATZOH

by Carol S. Lashof

SHAYNA *(to audience)* There's this dream I have sometimes: my mom wakes me up in the middle of the night. She says, "We have to run away. We have to escape." So, we go out into the street, me and my mom and dad and my little brother who's crying, and there's already a whole crowd of people walking down the middle of the street, kind of like a parade, but there's no music and everybody looks scared. Then somebody says, "The soldiers are coming! Run! Pharaoh will catch us!" When I'm awake, I know this dream is about something that happened a long time ago. In Egypt.

I remember the first time I heard the story. Well, I mean, the first time I *listened* to the story, because I hear it every year at Passover, I just don't always pay attention. I was in second grade. You're not supposed to share your lunches at school, but my friend Nikki and me, we always did …

(Back in second grade.)

NIKKI   I'll trade you half a tuna fish for half a peanut butter and jelly.

SHAYNA   Today I don't have peanut butter and jelly.

Art by Deborah Green

NIKKI	What do you mean you don't have peanut butter and jelly? You always have peanut butter and jelly.
SHAYNA	*(proudly)* Today, I have a hard-boiled egg and butter and matzoh. No bread.
NIKKI	Why don't you have bread?
SHAYNA	Because it's Passover.
NIKKI	So?
SHAYNA	So, we don't eat bread on Passover.
NIKKI	I'm eating bread.
SHAYNA	Because you're not Jewish. You're Christmas.
NIKKI	Silly. It's March. It's forever 'til Christmas. How long do you have to not eat bread?
SHAYNA	For eight days.
NIKKI	And you have to eat that other stuff, that cracker thing?
SHAYNA	It's matzoh.
NIKKI	Can I try it?
SHAYNA	I don't know. It might be against the rules or something. Because you're not Jewish.
NIKKI	Well … it looks gross anyway. It's kind of wrinkly. I'm glad I don't have to eat it.
SHAYNA	*(to audience)* After Nikki said it looked gross, well, it sort of started to taste gross, too. I ate my apple and my egg, but I didn't finish the matzoh. Nikki offered me one of her chocolate chip cookies, but I couldn't eat it because cookies are like bread and cake. You can't eat them during Passover. *(NIKKI exits)* That night when my mom was tucking me in, I asked her why.

(MOM enters.)

MOM	Because long ago, when the Jews were running away from Egypt, they didn't have time to let the bread dough rise. They had to cook it flat. That's matzoh.
SHAYNA	Why were they running away?
MOM	Because they wanted to be free. In Egypt, there was an evil ruler, a pharaoh, who forced them to be slaves. They had to work in the hot sun, all day, making bricks to build his cities, and if they were tired and didn't work fast enough, then they were whipped.
SHAYNA	How did they get away?
MOM	There was a brave leader named Moses—
SHAYNA	Like in the song?
MOM	Yes. Like in the song. Moses led the people out of Egypt. He led them to the edge of the sea. And then they were trapped. Or they thought they were. Pharaoh's soldiers were right behind them. But then something amazing happened: the sea opened up in front of them and the people walked across on dry land. When the soldiers tried to cross, too, the sea closed over them and they were drowned. At least, that's how the story goes.
SHAYNA	And that's why we eat matzoh?
MOM	Yes. That's why. To remember that we were slaves.
SHAYNA	So, if you're not Jewish, you can't eat matzoh, right?
MOM	Of course you can eat matzoh. Everybody can eat matzoh.
SHAYNA	Mom? Can I ask you something? *(SHAYNA whispers in MOM's ear. MOM smiles and nods, then exits)*

SHAYNA   *(to audience)* The next day I brought matzoh to school for my whole class.

(SHAYNA's teacher, MR. MATTHEWS, and the CLASS enter.)

MR. MATTHEWS   Can you tell us what's special about matzoh, Shayna?

NIKKI   It's good!

SHAYNA   Yeah, it's good! Also, it's flat. 'Cuz when you're running away from slavery, you can't wait for the bread to rise.

(NIKKI raises her hand. MR. MATTHEWS calls on her.)

MR. MATTHEWS   Nikki.

NIKKI   My great-great-great-grandmom, she couldn't wait for the bread to rise either. She ran away from slavery, too.

SHAYNA   Did she live in Egypt?

NIKKI   No. In Mississippi. She had to pick cotton all day in the hot sun for no money. And the slave masters, they were horrible and mean and they whipped her and stuff. So, one night, she ran away. She was all by herself and she was scared and she had to walk and walk and walk. But when she got across the river, then she was free.

SHAYNA   Did the soldiers chase her?

NIKKI   Not soldiers. Men with dogs. Bloodhounds. They almost caught her.

SHAYNA   *(to audience)* After that, Mr. Matthews said we could sing a Passover song. I wanted to sing "Go Down, Moses," and it turned out a lot of kids knew it already. Nikki said she sang it in her church, which I thought was kinda funny, but then Mr. Matthews explained that it was actually an African-American song. That when black people were slaves here in the United States they couldn't talk about how they wanted to be free, but they could talk and sing about Moses and Egypt and stuff. It was sort of like a code.

    That was in second grade. I'm in fifth grade now, but I still think about it a lot, the day my whole class ate matzoh and sang: "Let my people go … " And when I wake up in the middle of the night and I'm scared, it helps me to think about everyone singing together. Because you know what I think? I think if we're all here together, singing about freedom, then there won't be anybody left to be in Pharaoh's army, and we won't any of us have to run away at all anymore. We can stay right here.

(The cast sings "Go Down, Moses." The audience is encouraged to join in.)

ALL   When Israel was in Egypt land,
    Let my people go!
    They worked so hard they could not stand,
    Let my people go!

    Go down, Moses,
    Way down to Egypt land.
    Tell ol' Pharaoh:
    "Let my people go!"

AMERICA DIDN'T CRUMBLE

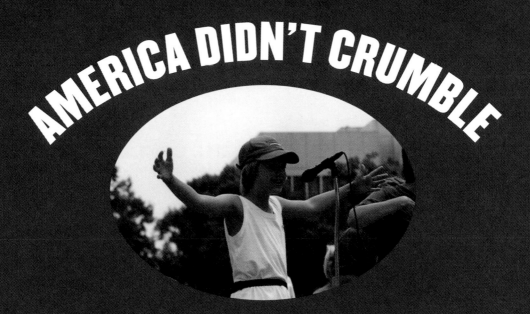

Excerpted from the testimony of Sol Kelley-Jones, ten years old, before the Wisconsin State Assembly Committee on Families and Children, March 10, 1997

Hi, my name is Sol Kelley-Jones. I am ten years old. I'm a really lucky kid because I have two moms who love me very much. They both take care of me, like cooking my meals, helping me with homework, making juice Popsicles when I'm sick, giving me hugs and playing games with me.

Some people don't understand everything about my family. Like, they ask me: "Who is your real mom?" I say: "They're both my real moms."

In my history class in school, we've been studying the Constitution of the United States. It says that all people are created equal and have the right for the pursuit of happiness and equal protection under the law.

We've also been learning about Elizabeth Freeman, who was an African-American slave, owned by one of the drafters of the Constitution. As a slave she didn't have any rights. Elizabeth Freeman couldn't get legally married and her kids could get taken away from her. Today, my two moms also can't get legally married. It's scary for me to know that if one of my parents died, I could be taken away from my other parent.

Two hundred years ago, Elizabeth Freeman went to the government and asked for her rights—like it said in the Constitution. But some people hated or feared African-Americans so much that they would have changed the Constitution, rather than allow Elizabeth Freeman her rights. They said terrible things, like if African-American people were freed and had equality under law, everything Americans believed in would crumble. Elizabeth Freeman won her freedom, the right to legally marry and to protect her children, and America didn't crumble ... it got better.

There are people today who say the same kinds of things about my family that they were saying about Elizabeth Freeman and her family.

They say things like: "God hates gays and lesbians." That our family is bad. This is scary for me. I don't want to be afraid of these people and I don't want them to be afraid of me. I think we can all get along. We don't have to be exactly the same way.

Not everyone is lucky enough to have two great parents, so I know I have a lot to be thankful for.

Photo by Holly Dunagan

COURAGE

Lyrics and music by Bob Blue

Music on page 151

A small thing once happened at school
That brought up a question for me
And somehow it forced me to see
The price that I pay to be cool.
Diane is a girl that I know
She's strange, like she doesn't belong
I don't mean to say that that's wrong
We don't like to be with her, though.
And so, when we all made a plan
To have this big party at Sue's
Most kids in the school got the news
But no one invited Diane.

The thing about Taft Junior High
Is, secrets don't last very long
I acted like nothing was wrong
When I saw Diane start to cry.
I know you may think that I'm cruel
It doesn't make me very proud
I just went along with the crowd—
It's sad, but you have to at school.
You can't pick the friends you prefer
You fit in as well as you can
I couldn't be friends with Diane
'Cuz then they would treat me like her.

In one class at Taft Junior High
We study what people have done
With gas chamber, bomber and gun
In Auschwitz, Japan and My Lai.
I don't understand all I learn
Sometimes I just sit there and cry
The whole world stood idly by
To watch as the innocent burned.
Like robots obeying some rule
Atrocities done by the mob
All innocent, doing their job
And what was it for? Was it cool?

The world was aware of this hell
But how many cried out in shame?
What heroes, and who was to blame?
A story that no one dared tell.
I promise to do what I can
To not let it happen again
To care for all women and men
I'll start by inviting Diane.

CREDO

by Norma L. Bowles, Sr.

I am a work-in-progress—

Part of an unfinished creation.

In me lies the promise of new achievements.

I am eager to experience the wonder

That will be expressed through me today.

How unique I am!

And how unique is each person I encounter.

Together we have a common destiny:

To make the world a better place in which to live.

With us rests the glowing prospect

Of co-existing in a happy, peaceful and loving world

With all the creatures of the Earth—

A prospect that has been beckoning to humanity

Since the beginning of time.

Art by James McMullan

MUSIC

It Takes All Kinds

Lyrics by Mark Waldrop
Music by Brad Ellis

Calypso

Moth - er Na - ture's pret - ty smart and she al - ways finds

That she likes va - ri - e - ty; it takes all kinds.

Do you like a peach - 's smooth wat - er - mel - on rinds?

Both are love - ly to the touch; it takes all kinds!

What good would a rain - bow be if it were on - ly

blue? What if ev' - ry - one you met

was a clone of you? Oooh!

Some crea - tures run or

jump or fly, some sit on their be - hinds;

Fast or slow, they go to show: it takes all kinds!

Look at lit - tle Em - i - ly; frill - y dress and

Bar - bie dolls; Check out lit - tle Bet - ty Sue.

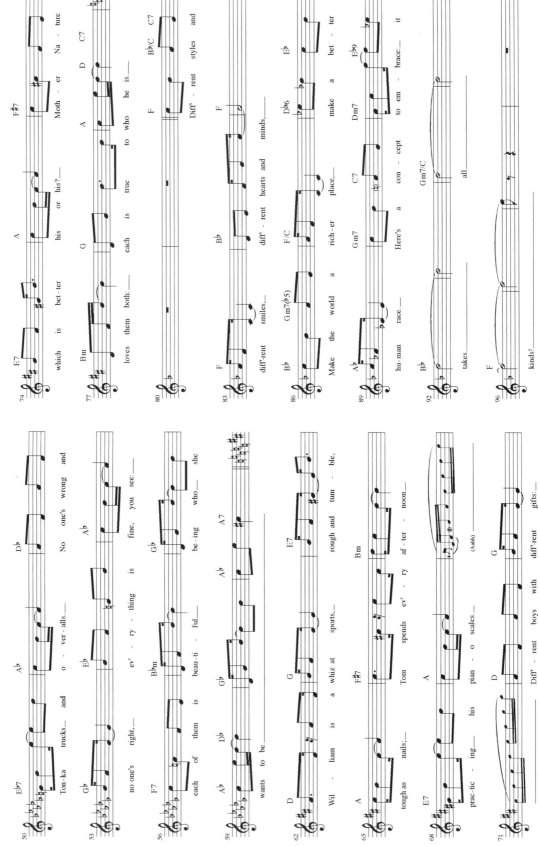

In Mommy's High Heels

Lyrics by Paul Selig
Music by Scott Killian

In Mommy's High Heels 3
32 E♭maj7 D♭dim Fm7 F7
on - ly brought two things I wear That make me hap - py,— make me tall.
34 Fm7 B♭ F♯dim B♭7 Slowly
They can laugh, but I'm a - bove them all: In
rit.
36 E♭ B♭
Mom - my's high heels the world is beau - ti - ful,
38 E♭ E♭7 A♭ B♭aug
Let the peas - ants choke way down be - low. I'm
40 E♭ E♭7 A♭ Fm7
stand - ing high a - bove the crowds, My head is break - ing through the clouds. In
accel.
42 Fm7/B♭
Mom - my's high heels— I'm ten feet tall!—
(♩ = 126)
44 E♭maj7
In
46
Mom - my's high heels life's a fan - ta - sy:
In Mommy's High Heels 4
48
Ev' - ry wish I make is a de - cree! Let
50
Sis - sy keep her shrunk - en heads, Let Ma - ry walk her dog who's dead. In my
52 Fm7/B♭
mom - my's high heels— I have it all!—
54
56 G♭
Here the world is beau - ti - ful:
58 A♭m/G♭
For - ests of coat racks and shoe trees, A
60 G♭
land of hope and shop - ping sprees!—
62 A Bm
— When I grow up, I'll

Given All I've Got

Music and lyrics by
Jayne Atkinson

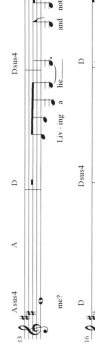
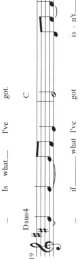

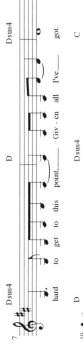

22
I can't live each day, turn - ing my
25
head a - way, Be-cause of what peo - ple fear, what
28
peo - ple will say. I've got to
31
stand up now, and hold my head up proud, And be a
34
bright-er life for a bright - er day.
37
There's so much I can
40
do, If I live my life in truth.
43
Help me throw the lies a - way. There's so much I want to

46
say.
49
I've worked so hard to get to this point,
52
Giv-en all I've got. But what is the point
55
if what I've got is - n't seen?
58
Liv-ing in life and liv-ing it free Is what I've
61
got. And that is the point of liv - ing at
64
all to be me. I can't
67
live each day, turn - ing my head a - way, Be-cause of

Same World

Music and Lyrics by
Jayne Atkinson and Katherine Reclusado

150

Courage

Words and Music by Bob Blue

* Additional verses may be found within the piece.

151

A SPECIAL THANK YOU

A heartfelt thanks to all the extraordinary people who have helped Fringe Benefits in the creation of *Cootie Shots*. This book would not exist without you.

For courageous and beautiful work, major gratitude to Director Laurie Woolery and the original cast and crew of *Cootie Shots*, which was performed for the first time in October 1999, at Highways Performance Space–Director of Development: Laura Jane Salvato; Technical Director/Lighting Designer: Jeff Cain; Music Director: Yvonne Regalado Flores; Costume Designer: Martha Ferrara; Assistant Costume Designer: Katrina Werner; Stitcher: Vicky Eagleson; Stage Manager: Patrick Williams; Assistant Stage Manager: Laura Nagata Murphy; Props: Eldon Cline, Willa Mamet, Mercedes Gilliom, Christopher Pennington, A. B. Franks and Jason Schomas; Music was performed and recorded by Robert Martson. Guitar performances in *My Friend Is Blue* and *Our Own Drum*: Jonathan Dyke. Music performance for *In Mommy's High Heels*: Scott Killian. Masks for *Snooty Patooty*: Ida Bagus Anom. The Ensemble: Stephen Allman, Dianne Carlin, Eldon Cline, Mark E. Rosenthal, Steven Christopher Ruiz, Krista Schafer, Tien Thai, Mercy Vasquez and Terrence Winston. Understudies: Laura Nagata Murphy and Patrick Williams.

Our deep appreciation goes as well to Tour Managers Stephen Allman and David N. Young (soon to be Rabbi Young), Stage Managers Dena Anderson, A. B. Franks and Allison Hall, and actors Tim Michael, Cristina Nava, Cynthia Ruffin and Anthony Yuro, who joined the show for our school tour.

We also wish to extend profound thanks to the following individuals whose generous financial contributions made *Cootie Shots* possible: Joyce Bader, Lloyd Botway, John H. Bowles., Norma Bowles, Sr., Pamela Brenna, Center for Gender Sanity, Elice J. Coe, Reverend Donn A. and Helen M. Crail, Teresa Cullen, Greg Dart, Joyce Elaine Davidson, Henry D. Delarosa, Barbara June Dodge, Deirdre A. Dooley, Thomas W. Dowell, Michael Engler, Cliff Faulkner, Katherine Gibbs and Keith Widaman, Barbara And Steven Grossman, Roger Henderson, Keith Hoshal and Christopher Laabs, Mary Jo Hunker, Tim Jacques, Mary Alice Jennings, Shirley M. Kennedy, Kathi Kent, Daisietta Kim, Neil S. and Robin S. Kramer, Deborah A. Markoe, Loring McAlpin, Marjorie And Robert Middleton, Martin and Margaret Olson, Maureen O'Toole, Kirk A. Pemberton, Sarah Pillsbury, William G. and Dolores P. Rice, Michael and Nancy Riordan, Mark R. and Linda K. Rodgers, Anne Rowland, Michele and Robert Rivero, Kate Solow, Joan Soloway, Eric L. Stone, Hendricus Struijk, Caroli Waynick, Lauren Weingarten, Pamela Weymouth, Melvin E. and Lucile M. Wheatley, Jr., Sarah D. Woodbury and Kenneth Zahner.

For always going the extra mile, through thick and through thin, very special thanks to Laura Jane Salvato, Sonja Seaver, Susan Jonas, Stacie Chaiken, M. Michele Manzella Rivero, Bob Rivero, Danielle Usry, Karen Ocamb, The Gutierrez Family, Shishir Kurup, Debbie Michels, Steven Christopher Ruiz, Jerry Battey, Alan Pulner and About Productions, Steven Hicks and GLSEN/L.A., Chris Evans and GALIC/UTLA, Gail Rolf and Project 10, Torie Osborn and the staff, Board and members of the Liberty Hill Foundation, Mary Milelcek and Highways Performance Space, Robin Lithgow and the Los Angeles Unified School District, Rosa Furumoto and the staff and mothers of Sharp Avenue Elementary School's Every Child A Learner program, Marta M. Franco and the staff and mothers of San Fernando Elementary School's Pedagogy for Accelerated Learning program, Helen Cohen and Women's Educational Media, Carol S. Lashof, Jaime Wolfe, Jane Abernethy, James Williams, Seana Magee, Kate Solow, Stephen Allman, Eldon Cline, Cristina Nava, Cynthia Ruffin, Dianne Carlin, Krista Schafer, Barbara June Dodge, Daisietta Kim, Jan Tattam, A. B. Franks, Fran Hynds, Kenneth Zahner, Keith Hoshal, Christopher Laabs and Norma Bowles, Sr.

For invaluable input and support at just the right time, special thanks to Lynn Bielefelt, Virginia Stevens, Marilyn Matevia, Eva Eilenberg, Eric L. Stone, Dan Horn, Vincent O'Donohue, Liane Schirmer, Tina Schoen, Sylvia Rhue, Mady Schutzman, Father Chris Rosales, SDB, Seth Cutler, Cathy Figel, Bryan Edney, Deb Nishimura, Uncle Ruthie, Bob Blue, Kathleen McHugh, Tim Miller, Dena Anderson, Claudia Martinez, Todd Nelson, Norman Frisch, Viv Varela, Chon Noriega, Ron Scapp, Kirk Bell, John D'Emilio, Sharon Grady, Chris Cook, Aarone Beronacci , Marcia Meyers, Kate Mendeloff, Sheila Hillinger, John Hazatone, Joanie Martin, Chiray Koo, Dr. Evangelina R. Stockwell, Viki L. Montera, Ed.D., Carol Bernstein, Mark Mask, Judy Bogart, Diane Kahn-Epstein, Michael and Nancy Riordan, Amy Armstrong, Soraya Sarhaddi Nelson, Leslie Bentley, Amadeu J. Pavini, Lorenzo Gonzalez, B.C. Keller, Mark Templin, Mike Quiroz, Tania Myren, Free to Be … Foundation, Carl Weintraub of We Tell Stories, Chris Bellerive and Lynn Hunt, Steven Argila, Mike Marden, all the production volunteers from Norma's acting classes at SCR, and to Miriah Rifkin and her 1998–1999 4th grade class at Murray Elementary School.

For most delicious photography, many thanks to Kathi Kent, *Kyodo News*; Joanne Lange, Mary Pierce and Kate Solow. Special Thanks as well to Boris Sinelnikov at Photo Delight in West Hollywood.

For "just the ticket" videography, thanks to Janice Engel and Cobalt Films, Stacie Chaiken and Pat Pahrens, videographers; Michael Hofacre, editor; and the folks at Media One.

For a Godsend donation of rehearsal space, gratitude to Patricia Shelhamer and the Family Assistance Program and Cristina Nava and Prospect of Art.

For life-saving donations of fiscal services, major thanks to Kinde Durkee of Durkee & Associates, and Jerry Battey and the Friends of EAGLES Academy, Inc. .

Very special thanks to the students from the following schools and community and religious organizations at which Cootie Shots was performed before this book went to press. We loved all your beautiful pictures and thoughtful letters and comments! Special thanks, also, to all the teachers and administrators for welcoming us into your schools and for mailing us the students' drawings and writings! The Accelerated School, Alamo Elementary School, The Alexandria House Program, Aviva SAFE Program, Badger Springs Middle School, Bay Area Discovery Museum, Berkeley Arts Magnet, Berkeley Unified School District, Berkwood Hedge Elementary, The Blazers Youth Service Community Club, Inc., Canfield Elementary, Caroldale Learning Community, Central American Resource Center, Cheramoya Elementary School, Children's Day School, City Terrace Elementary, Clover Avenue School, Commonwealth Elementary School, Cragmont Elementary, Crossroads School, Delavan Drive Elementary School, Eagle Rock Elementary School, El Morro School, Fifty-Second Street School, Foundations School Community, Franklin Microsociety Magnet School, Golden Gate Elementary School, Halldale Avenue School, Hawaiian Avenue Elementary School, Hobart Boulevard Elementary School, Horace Mann Elementary School, International Performing Arts Festival for Youth, John Muir School, Kehillat Israel, La Salle Avenue School, Loreto Street Elementary School, Los Angeles Children's Museum, Marin Country Day School, Marquez Charter School, Martin Luther King Middle School, Mar Vista Elementary School, Melrose Avenue Elementary School, The Mirman School, Murray Elementary School, Nora Sterry School, The Oaks School, The Open Charter School, Orange County Human Relations Steinberg Leadership Conference, Palma Ceia Elementary, Pleasant Valley School, Polytechnic Lower School, PS #1, Ramona Elementary School, Rockdale Elementary School, Rosewood Elementary School, San Ramon Elementary School, Santa Monica Alternative School House, San Fernando Elementary School, Selma Avenue Elementary School, Sharp Avenue Elementary School, Signal Hill Elementary School, St. Thomas the Apostle Elementary School, South Coast Repertory's Young Conservatory, South Gate Middle School, South Shore Magnet School, St. Martin in the Fields Elementary School, Sunshine Gardens School, Temple Israel, Thirty-Second Street Elementary School, Thomas Jefferson Elementary School, Toluca Lake Elementary School, Top of the World Elementary School, Vista School, Warner Avenue Elementary School, Washington Elementary School, and the Westerley School of Long Beach!

More than 500 individuals, organizations and schools collaborated to create the plays, songs, poems and artwork that comprise Cootie Shots. We can't thank you enough!

Dramaturgs: Stephen Allman, Carl Andress, Adam Behrman, Norma Bowles, Lynn Capri, Stacie Chaiken, Seth Cutler, John D'Emilio, Barbara June Dodge, Mercedes Gilliom, Steven Hicks, David Lee Kelting, Carol S. Lashof, Vicky Lewis, Willa Mamet, Deborah Markoe, Kathleen McHugh, Alan Pulner, Gail Rolf, Mark E. Rosenthal, Sonja Seaver, Kate Solow, Pamela Weymouth and Laurie Woolery.

Play Development Workshop Leaders: Norma Bowles, Robi Guillen, Claudia Martinez, Alan Pulner, Mark E. Rosenthal and Steven Christopher Ruiz.

The following artists, educators, therapists, parents and youth collaborated with Fringe Benefits outside workshop settings to create the text of Cootie Shots: Jehan F. Agrama, Azzam A. Ahmad, Luis Alfaro, Carl Andress, Billy Aronson, Jayne Atkinson, John Belluso, Bea Bernstein, Bob Blue, Jeudi Cornejo Brealey, Joseph Brouillette, Tony Carbone, Stacie Chaiken, Debra Chasnoff, Jennifer Clarvoe, Helen S. Cohen, Barbara June Dodge, Lily Dodge Dart, Lucia Dodge Dart, Brad Ellis, John Fleck, Dana Gallagher, Jesus Garcia, Forrest Hartl, Sheila Hillinger, Jamice Lamara Jefferson, Michael Kearns, Sol Kelley-Jones, Scott Killian, Shishir Kurup, Elaine Laron, Carol S. Lashof, Christopher Liam Moore, Kristina Olsen, Mark Piatelli, Katherine Reclusado, Father Cris Rosales, SDB, Paul Selig, Marsha Lee Sheiness, Smile, Bernardo Solano, Paula Weston Solano, Anna, Lewis and Nicky Solow-Collins, Eric Stegman, Alice Tuan, Johnny Valentine, Mark Waldrop, Chris Wells, Michele Williams and Yubiani.

The following contributors collaborated in workshops held at the homes of Alan Pulner, Mark E. Rosenthal, Deborah Markoe and Yvonne Golomb, Barbara Babchick and Margie Haber, and Stephen Allman and Adam Behrman: Stephen Allman, Anonymous, John Arnau, Barbara Babchick, Kelly Bates, Adam Behrman, Norma L. Bowles, Sr., Dena Brabender, Robert Campion, Lynn Capri, Dianne Carlin, Stacie Chaiken, Miki Chase, Bert Christensen, Leigh Curran, Seth Cutler, Marie Defais, Werner DeLaFayette, Nancy Alicia De Los Santos, Thalia Ferry, Yvonne Golomb, Robert Grace, Robi Guillen, Julian, Lydia, Michael and Natalie Gutierrez, Margie Haber, Chris Haiss, Kirstin Hartenbower, Joe Herrera, Sarah Himmelheber, Peter Howard, Kris Hurst, Laryssa Husiak, Michele Kammerer, Kathi Kent, Jennifer Kingsley, Andrew and Marilee Kuhlman, Cassandra Lewis, Ferdinand Lewis, Aurelio Locsin, Steve Ludwig, Deborah Markoe, Joanie Martin, Claudia Martinez, Jamie Meyer, Debbie Michels, Luis A. Pena, Alan Pulner, Catharine Ramos, Natalie Romana, Melissa Reynolds,

Mark E. Rosenthal, Cynthia Ruffin, Steven Christopher Ruiz, Erika Sloane, Barbara Speck, Kate Solow, Jan Tattam, Leilani Tolbert, Joe Walsh, Janis Walworth, Billie Weiser, Amity Westcott and Laurie Woolery.

Ms. Langley's 1st Grade Leaders at Thirty-Second Street Visual and Performing Arts/Math/Science/Technology, Teaching Assistant Emma Benitez: Dennis Argueta, Anna Brancaccio, Marlene Briones, Lauren Cannell, Sharon Cespedes, Candice Cho, Roxanne Flores, Leslie Guzman, Heela Kang, Justina Lee, Antoine Louis, Jr., Daniel Martin, Meshach Puerto, Aneiki Randolph, James Robinson, Arianna Sanchez and Barbara Silva.

Lynn Capri's 4th and 5th Grade Students at Foundations School Community: Jon E. Brown, Melissa Cober, Baylee Dovall, Conner Kelly-Eiding, A. J. Erickson, Deanna Herbert, Ariane Lange and Ari Marcos.

James Williams's 5th Grade Student at Halldale Avenue Elementary School: Christian Watkins.

Arlene Karon's 3rd Grade Students at Nora Sterry Elementary, Assistant Teacher Anne Marie Fierro: Yasmin Antonio, Michael Carpio, Bianca Lagunas, David Lee, Levi Mock, Donald W. Moss, Jr., Christian M. Ray, Sheena Rice, Joshua Romero, LaTearea Tatam, Georgette Townson, Prentiss Westbrooks and Monique Williamson.

Katie Safford's 3rd Grade Students at Ivanhoe Elementary, Assistant Teacher Karen Trujillo: Courtney Blackburn, Raphael Martin Chua, Alex Dye, Paolo Everett, Flannery Hunter, Stacy Kim, Andrew Mori, James Schulps, Cameron Shubb, Lewis Solow-Collins, Dazie White and Megan Willoughby.

Crossroads School FLAG group: Adam Behrman, Bianca Bracho-Perez, Liz Carlisle, Emily Forman, Mercedes Gilliom, Vignette Hart, Matt Kellard, Jamie Meyer, Ann-Sophie Morrissette and Miranda Robin.

PFLAG/Los Angeles: Bea Bernstein, Dianne Carlin, Lydia and Michael Gutierrez, Kathi Kent, Deborah Markoe, Pirate Princess Poppy, Mike Strickland and Sylvia Weisenberg. (Norma Bowles regrets having misplaced the complete list of workshop participants.)

PFLAG/South Bay: Joan Atkinson, Craig Block, Joyce Cannon, Virginia Helker, Sarah Himmelheber, Rev. Robert J. Klein, Kristie Lanktree, Linda and Randy Patton, Mark E. Rosenthal, Steven Christopher Ruiz, Gina Russo, Debra Shrader, Shannon Shue, John F. Smith and Jan Tattam.

PFLAG/South Orange: Jillian Buschauer, Bob Crowder, Alan Davis, Ellen Dowd, June Hansen, Lynn and Alex Hunt, Laryssa Husiak, Kathi Kent, Cassandra Lewis, Jerry O'Brian, Pirate Princess Poppy, Peter Sharpe, Bec Soles, Joan Soloway, Jan Tattam and Mel and Lucile Wheatley.

PFLAG/Ventura: Lois Story, Kathi Kent, Nanette, Richard and Tom Benbrook. (Norma Bowles regrets having misplaced the complete list of workshop participants.)

Jeffrey Griffith's Gay and Lesbian Youth Center: J.A.A., Derek Babineaux, Star Barboza, Joshua Beach, Baby Brown Eyes, Pia Burns, V. Camille, Preston Czifra, Allowishes Ullyseus Fernandez, Leslie Ann Harper, Tyler Lequan Harris, Gabriel Miguel Hernandez, Sarah Himmelheber, Elias Jimenez, Gazelle Linton, Casey Lisbon, Miguel Lopez, G.E.M., Jason Manley, Anthony Marquez, Claudia Martinez, Tito Maurice, Jose Mejia, Jenn Millar, Juan Morales, Jorge Moreno, Jeffrey Todd Pranter, A.K.A. Quazi, Jose Louis Ramirez, Duane Renfro, Roxann, Shassy, Ivey Jean Siddens, Sheila Sousa, Steffanie Stewarts, Kateeb Tariq, David Telford, Cassandra Weathers and James T. Williams.

EAGLES Academy: Alex Avila, Domingo Bara, Juan Bautista, Miguel Bonilla, Eddie Bushnell, Luis Alberto Chavez, Chuckie, Kenia Covarrubias, Dorrie Cox, Maria de la Cueva, J.R. Dollar, Refugia Galinda, Victor Garcia, Ginger, Marlyn Gonzalez, Robi Guillen, Jorge Hernandez, Robert Hernandez, Noppol Hunsungnoen, Mark Imme, Ivory, Anthony Johnson, Nashika Johnson, Christina Killings, Micheol Klarc, Ryan Linares, Lollie, Miguel (Alexia) Lopez, Rebecca Lopez, Freddie Love, Karen Mazariegos, Mystery, Dileytt Oropesa, Raul Oropesa, Rosie Padilla, Rafaelita Lilah Parra, Tresvon Patterson, Jorge Peñate, Gloria Pinzon, Pogo Robledo, Ronnie Rodgers, Roz, Andy Ruiz, Denise Salas, Nicolas Sanchez, Oscar Sandoval, Frank Talamantes, Curtis Taylor, Dominique Vargas, Eva Odette Vargas, Christian Villanueva, Patrick Williams and Renee Zeleaya.

Contributing Visual Artists: Sam Alper, Kim Bach, Fanny Ballentine-Himberg, Naniqui Bernardez, Dan Bielefelt, Ned Bittinger, Peter Brooke, Debra Chasnoff, Hayley Chin, Anna Cohen, Helen S. Cohen, Siena Ko Colombier, Corbis, Holly Dunagan, Rebeca Escala-Viñas, Martha Ferrara, Alex Fink, Fayzan Gowani, Deborah Green, C. M. Gross, Barbara Grzeslo, Keith Haring, Lemond Harris, Margaret M. Hartley, Lazavier James, Lynn Jeffries, Helen Ju, Flor Juarez, Tia Kearns, Kathi Kent, Suk Gyu Sean Kim, Madison Wells Kimbro, Mark Tapio Kines, Joanne Lange, Justina Lee, Albert Llanos, Pilar Lopez, Daniel Martin, Lily McGarr, James McMullan, Avery Miller, Chris Müller, Christopher Myers, Zachary Nicita, Kitty Oakes, Mayumi Oda, Pirate Princess Poppy, Rose Portillo, Meshach Puerto, James C. Ransome, Norman Rockwell, Arianna Sanchez, Lynette Schmidt, Helen Shen, Smithsonian Institution (National Anthropological Archives), Anna Solow-Collins, Nicky Solow-Collins, Kitty Suen, Sosseh Taimoorian, Ashley Treacy, Adan Valdez, Gabrielle Veit-Bermúdez, Betty Villalobos, Andy Warhol, Kendra Wohlert, Lauren Yoshikawa, Beiji "Jimmy" Zhang.

ARTIST BIOGRAPHIES

We want to thank the many people who contributed their work to this book:

(All pieces were created in arrangement with Fringe Benefits for the purpose of production or publication in this volume, except where noted. All reprinted or excerpted material appears here by permission, with full cite provided on copyright page. All photos throughout the volume were taken by Norma Bowles unless otherwise noted.)

Writers:

Jehan F. Agrama is an Arab-American Muslim, born in Cairo, Egypt. She attended school in Rome, Italy, and came to the U.S. in 1976 to attend Pomona College, where she received a bachelor's degree in mathematics. She holds an honors M.B.A. from Pepperdine's Presidential Key Executive Program. She is a founder of the Gay and Lesbian Alliance Against Defamation/ Los Angeles (GLAAD/LA). She has been married with children to Dwora Fried for more than eighteen years.

Azzam A. Ahmad is an architect, writer and dancer born in Lebanon and raised in Kuwait. He worked for the Kuwait Oil Company as a design engineer. Mr. Ahmad contributed the concept and design for *Dream of War* at Pratt Institute. He has written for the Joseph Campbell Foundation newsletter.

Luis Alfaro is a peformer and writer of poetry, plays, short stories, solo performance and journalism. A Chicano born and raised in the Pico-Union district of downtown Los Angeles, he is the recipient of the MacArthur "genius" Fellowship and an NEA/TCG Playwrights Fellowship.

Carl Andress lives in New York City. His credits as both actor and director include: *Queen Amarantha* at the WPA, *Shanghai Moon* at Theatre for the New City (both in New York City) and *Die! Mommy! Die!* at the Coast Playhouse in Los Angeles. He toured internationally in AFT's *Aladdin*. Mr. Andress is a graduate of the University of New Hampshire.

Billy Aronson is a playwright anthologized in *Best American Short Plays 1992–93* and *Plays from Woolly Mammoth.* His work is performed frequently at New York City's Ensemble Studio Theatre. He created the original concept and additional lyrics for *Rent*. His TV writing includes scripts for Children's Television Workshop, Nickelodeon and MTV.

Jayne Atkinson is an actress who has appeared in theatre, film and television. She has been writing and performing music with Fringe Benefits since 1991.

Joan Atkinson, mother of seven, loves children and people. Called "Mom" by many who come her way in need of a loving family, Joan looks for the beauty inside each person and is never disappointed.

John Belluso is currently the NEA/TCG Playwright-in-Residence at Trinity Rep, and has recently been commissioned to write a new children's play for the Salt Lake City 2002 Olympic Committee. His plays have been seen in venues such as Perishable Theatre, Ensemble Studio Theatre and the Mark Taper Forum.

Bea Bernstein, a recent octogenarian, is a founding member of the Federation (1981) and L.A. PFLAG (1976) and is the first non-gay person to serve on the board of the L.A. Gay and Lesbian Community Services Center.

Bob Blue has written hundreds of songs. He has also written and produced several children's plays. Now, on a disability retirement, he volunteers in an elementary school and continues to write.

Kate Bornstein is the author of *My Gender Workbook* and *Gender Outlaw*, which is currently being used in more than eighty colleges. A transgendered writer and performer, Kate wants everybody to understand that gender is a rainbow spectrum.

Norma L. Bowles, Sr. is a widowed mother of four who farms in the Santa Ynez Valley. She is a 1942 graduate of Bryn Mawr College. She is a science writer (*Psi Search*, Harper & Row, 1978); exhibition producer (Psi SEARCH–Smithsonian Institution Traveling Exhibition Services 1975–79) and lecturer. Ms. Bowles is active in fundraising for science scholarships and supporting environmental and educational initiatives.

Jeudi Cornejo Brealey is an interdisciplinary artist/writer working in film, theatre, cabaret and photography. Drawing inspiration form her Costa Rican and Mexcan-American heritage, she focuses on themes of family, identity and spirit. She lives with her family in Southern California.

Joseph Brouillette is the author of numerous plays, screenplays and short stories. His play, *20 Questions*, ran at the Tamarind and Coast theatres in Los Angeles and *Young Man* premiered in Los Angeles in the fall of 2000. He is writing his first novel.

Liz Carlisle wrote *The Princess Petunia* while in high school. She was raised in Los Angeles, graduated from the Crossroads School in 1999 and is currently attending Cornell University in Ithaca.

Stacie Chaiken was a contributor to and workshop participant in Fringe Benefits' *Turn It Around!* She is the author of *A Wish Book* and *Looking for Louie*, a solo play which she also performs, about a a Russian, Jewish-American who goes off in search of her great-grandfather.

Debra Chasnoff is the Director of Women's Educational Media in San Francisco. She produced and directed *Deadly Deception: General Electric, Nuclear Weapons, and Our Environment*, which won the 1991 Academy Award for Best Documentary Short Subject. In 1996, she directed and co-produced (with Helen S. Cohen) *It's Elementary: Talking About Gay Issues in School*, which won numerous awards and continues to be distributed widely to schools, universities and community service organizations throughout the world. She is a graduate of Wellesley College with a degree in economics.

Helen S. Cohen is Senior Producer at Women's Educational Media in San Francisco, and is Executive Producer of Respect For All, a three-part media curriculum dealing with diversity issues for elementary and middle school children. She co-produced (with Debra Chasnoff) the acclaimed and internationally distributed *It's Elementary: Talking About Gay Issues in School.* She holds a master's degree in urban planning from MIT.

Nancy Alicia de Los Santos, a screenwriter, was the associate producer on the feature films *My Family* and *Selena*. She has written for *Latina Magazine* and *LatinGirl*. *Hispanic Magazine* named her one of the *"Ten to Watch"* in Hollywood.

Barbara June Dodge is Faculty Coordinator for CalArts' Community Arts Partnership/Plaza de la Raza Youth Theatre Program. She is a faculty member of the Cotsen Puppetry Center, based at CalArts. She has been on the faculty of South Coast Repertory Theatre's Young Conservatory, and is currently an artist-in-residence at a Santa Ana elementary school.

Brad Ellis is a composer who writes for stage, film and TV. He has conducted twelve albums on the Varese Sarabande label. Mr. Ellis served as the long-time Music Director of *Forbidden Broadway* in New York and Los Angeles.

John Fleck is an award-winning performance artist, writer and actor. His work has been seen at the Cannes Film Festival, the Museum of Contemporary Art, the New York Shakespeare Festival, among others. He is also one of the "NEA 4," who spearheaded a national campaign against artistic repression and won their court case against the federal government.

Dana Gallagher is the Director of Lights On Productions, a not-for-profit organization whose mission is to teach conflict resolution through educational theatre. She also provides training to youth and adults in the areas of interpersonal communication, conflict resolution and health education.

The Gutierrez Family lives in Elysian Valley, Los Angeles. They are advocates for gay rights. Mike works as a line man for Pacific Bell, Lydia works as a data processor/operator. At the time of *Doing the Right Thing*, Natalie was in the 7th grade at St. Theresa of Avila and her brother Julian was in the 11th grade at EAGLES Academy.

Sheila Hillinger is the Director of the Young Conservatory at South Coast Repertory in Costa Mesa, and has run her own Children's Theatre Company for the past twelve years. A public school theatre teacher for twenty years, in 1997 she was named Orange County Teacher of the Year and one of the top five teachers in California.

Peter Howard is an actor, writer and teacher. He is a founding member of Cornerstone Theater Company, and works in the youth arts programs of the National Conference for Community and Justice.

Laryssa Husiak was theatre major at Los Angeles County High School for the Arts when she co-wrote *Rapunzel*.

Mark Imme was seventeen years old when he co-wrote *The War of the Stuck-up Noses*. He lives in Los Angeles, and plans to become an actor and writer.

Jamice Lamara Jefferson (J.J.) was in 8th grade at the Westerly School in Long Beach, when she co-wrote *The Birthday Party.* J.J. lives with her mom and stepfather. Her Aunt Dorothy also cares for her, and lives in Compton, where J.J. was living at the time of the story.

Michael Kearns is a theatre artist and author of three books: *T-Cells & Sympathy*, *Acting = Life* and *Getting Your Solo Act Together*. He lives in Los Angeles with his daughter Tia.

Sol Kelley-Jones, fourteen, is the daughter of Joann Kelley and Sunshine Jones of Madison, WI. At ten, she testified at a legislative hearing against a bill prohibiting same sex marriage. The following year, she developed a multimedia presentation for elementary school students presenting positive images of lesbian, gay, bisexual and transgender people. In 1998, she was named Young Civil Libertarian of the Year by the Wisconsin ACLU and Young Feminist of the Year by the Wisconsin chapter of NOW.

Scott Killian composes music for theatre, dance, film and TV, including several children's videos with William Wegman. He lives in New York City with his partner of seven years and their two cats.

Tony Kushner is the author of *Angels in America* (Parts One and Two), *A Bright Room Called Day* and *Slavs!* His current projects include *Homebody/Kabul*, *Henry Box Brown or The Mirror of Slavery*, *St. Cecilia or The Power of Music* and *Caroline or Change*. He is the recipient of numerous awards, including the Pulitzer Prize and two Tony Awards for *Angels in America*. He grew up in Lake Charles, Louisiana, and lives in New York.

Carol S. Lashof is the author of several plays for both adults and young people. She has taught at Saint Mary's College, Moraga, CA, since 1983. She is a member of the Dramatists Guild. Ms. Lashof lives in Berkeley with her husband and their two daughters. She would like to acknowledge Shevra Tait, Dina Tait Barker and Amy Morton.

Miguel Lopez was sixteen and in the 10th grade at EAGLES Academy in Hollywood at the time he wrote *Mariposas.*

Christopher Liam Moore is a founding member of Cornerstone Theater Company. He lives in Los Angeles with his husband of sixteen years, Bill Rauch, their son Liam and their two golden retrievers.

José Louis Ramirez plans to become a childcare social worker so that he can help gay and lesbian adolescents and children.

Katherine Reclusado is the President of Chanting Rock Music. She is a singer/songwriter, artist, photographer, filmmaker and healer.

Father Cris Rosales is a Salesian of Don Bosco, a Catholic religious order of men who dedicate themselves to the service of the young. Father Cris has been teaching for eighteen years.

Cynthia Ruffin is an actor and writer from Montreal who currently resides in Echo Park.

Paul Selig is a playwright and librettist whose work includes the plays: *Mystery School* and *Terminal Bar*, and the operas: *Red Tide* and *Lamentations*. He is Director of the M.F.A. in Writing Program at Goddard College.

Paula Weston Solano was an overweight and often ostracized, mixed-race child living in a predominantly Anglo suburb. Though some kids hurt her feelings by calling her names and leaving her out of activities, Paula's teachers and friends saw her as a loving, smart, creative person. Now, she uses all her experiences as fuel for her writing and acting.

Erik R. Stegman is a political science major at Whittier College near Los Angeles. He plans to go to law school to become a civil rights attorney. He is a member of the National Board of Directors for the Gay, Lesbian and Straight Education Network (GLSEN).

Alice Tuan is the author of *Last of the Suns*, *Ikebana*, *Some Asians* and *New Culture for a New Country*. She has taught English as a Second Language in China and in the Los Angeles area. She has facilitated playwriting workshops for teenage wards of the California Youth Authority and high school students.

Johnny Valentine, winner of the Lambda Literary Award for *The Duke Who Outlawed Jelly Beans*, has written four books about children with gay and lesbian parents for Alyson Publications: *The Day They Put a Tax on Rainbows*; *The Daddy Machine*; *One Dad, Two Dads, Brown Dad, Blue Dad*; and *Two Moms, the Zark, and Me*.

Mark Waldrop is a writer, director and lyricist who lives in New York City.

Chris Wells is a theatre artist from Los Angeles. Mr. Wells developed *Liberty!* at the Actors' Gang Theatre with his friend Bridget Carpenter. *Liberty!* is touring the U.S. and being made into a movie.

Amity Westcott is a writing composition teacher. Her theatrical experience includes various writing, acting and directing projects as a founding member of Southern California's New Voices Playwrights' Workshop.

Pamela Weymouth is an Associate Clinical Social Worker who works with victims of domestic violence at the CalWorks Office of W.O.M.A.N., Inc. in San Francisco. She is a writer and poet.

Michele Williams was born and raised in Berkeley, where she now lives with her husband and their three children. She teaches 2nd grade and kindergarten.

Visual Artists:

Kim Bach is a Bay Area oil painter, exhibition curator and lesbian single mother. She was art curator for "A Conversation with Koko," a film about Koko and Michael, gorillas who sign and paint. Her paintings have been included in exhibitions at Villa Montalvo in Saratoga, CA; Christensen Heller Gallery in Oakland; and Henri Gallery in Washington, DC.

Dan Bielefelt made his home in San Francisco from 1972 until he died of AIDS in May 2000. A retrospective of his work was shown in San Francisco in 2001. A lifelong devotee of theatre and an enthusiastic supporter of *Cootie Shots*, his family and friends are delighted to contribute Dan's work to this project, in his memory.

Ned Bittinger is an award-winning portrait painter who also paints figurative scenes, landscapes and illustrations. His work has been shown in many galleries and in countless publications, including books for Scholastic, Inc. He has a Master of Fine Arts degree from George Washington University.

Peter Brooke, a native of England, began his professional career as a sculptor at Jim Henson's Creature Shop in London. His own works in bronze have been widely exhibited in the U.S. and abroad. He now lives in Los Angeles.

Holly Dunagan is a professional website developer who delights in photography. She's known Sol Kelley-Jones since she was a baby, and enjoys documenting her youth activism.

Martha Ferrara is an award-winning designer of more than seventy-five productions in theatre, dance, opera, video and performance art. She is perhaps best known for her 1980 interpretive reconstruction of costumes for Robert Benedetti's production of Malevich's 1913 *Victory Over the Sun*. She is Costume Director at CalArts.

Deborah Green lives in Berkeley with her daughter and dog. She received a B.F.A. from California College of Arts and Crafts in 1985. She was one of the illustrators for the Hesperian Foundation book, *A Book for Midwives*; and illustrated the cover of St. Martin's Press's *Building a Community of Learners*. She is the art teacher at Beacon Day School in Oakland.

C. M. Gross is a painter and photo-illustrator. Ms. Gross's work is in several permanent museum collections, including the Museum of The City of New York. Born and raised in Brooklyn, she is an assistant professor at Pratt Institute in the Communications Design Department.

Barbara Grzeslo is a graphic designer, illustrator and artist who lives and works in New York.

Keith Haring was born on May 4, 1958, and was raised in a Pennsylvania Dutch farm community. From a very early age (less than a year old) he took to drawing, copying alongside his cartoonist father. He attended the Pittsburgh Center for the Arts where he was given his first solo show, and in 1978 transferred to the School of Visual Arts in New York City. In New York he became inspired by graffiti art found on the streets and in the subway system. It is this influence which marked what is now his world-famous, bold artistic style and powerful images of social consciousness. He died of AIDS on February 16, 1990.

Lynn Jeffries is a set and costume designer and a founding member of Cornerstone Theater Company. She is now creating artwork for a book about her brother's cat, Fred.

Helen Ju is a freelance costume designer, draper, pattern-maker and stitcher; watercolorist; graphic illustrator; and website designer.

Kathi Kent is an editorial photographer working in Southern California. She has spent most of her career photographing sports, theatre and news. She has two daughters and spends her free time volunteering for children's charities.

Mark Tapio Kines graduated from CalArts in 1992, and works as both film director and graphic artist. He completed his first feature film *Foreign Correspondents* in 1999, and is currently developing his next film *Sharky Baby*. Mr. Kines is the art director of Paramount Pictures' online division.

James McMullan was born in Tsingato, North China, where his grandparents founded an Anglican mission. He was educated in China, India, Canada, and graduated from the Pratt Institute in 1958. His work has appeared in countless publications, and he serves as principal artist for Lincoln Center, where he has created dozens of play posters. He initiated the High Focus Drawing Program at the School for Visual Arts and has written numerous books on the art of illustration.

Chris Müller is an exhibit designer and illustrator who lives in Brooklyn.

Christopher Myers is a graduate of Brown University and the Whitney Museum of American Art Independent Studio Program. He received a Caldecott Medal honorary mention for his art in *Harlem* (Scholastic Press, Inc.). He is a freelance illustrator and painter, who lives in New York City.

Mayumi Oda is a painter and printmaker, who was raised near Tokyo in a Buddhist family. She continues to practice Zen. Her work is part of the collections at the Museum of Modern Art, the Library of Congress and the Tokyo University of Fine Art, from where she graduated. She is founder of the Plutonium Free Future organization in Berkeley and Tokyo.

Pirate Princess Poppy shimmers through life in San Francisco. There she attends college(s) and flexes her ninja skills as a feminist, artist, poet, healer, nanny, scone-maker and pixie. She plots trips to countries that begin with the letter "I" and dreams of a hooded fleecy sweater with bunny ears.

Rose Portillo is an actor/writer/director/visual artist, whose acting career began with a lead role in Luis Valdez's *Zoot Suit* (L.A., Broadway, feature film). Ms. Portillo is Associate Director of About Productions, an interdisciplinary theatre company. She teaches theatre and playwriting through A.S.K. Playwrights in the Schools, The Playwrights Project and Plaza de la Raza, among others.

James E. Ransome is a two-time Coretta Scott King Award-winning illustrator. He has a B.A. in illustration from the Pratt Institute, and was a student of the Art Students League. He has illustrated numerous children's books, and his work has appeared in many magazines.

Norman Rockwell was born in New York City in 1894. At fourteen, he enrolled at the New York School of Art, and continued his study at the Art Students League. While in his teens, he was hired as art director of *Boy's Life* (the official publication of the Boy Scouts). At twenty-two he painted his first cover for *The Saturday Evening Post*. Throughout his forty-seven-year association with the *Post*, he painted 321 covers.

Following the *Post* tenure in the 1960s, he began a ten-year relationship with *Look* magazine, painting topical pictures that illustrated his concerns about civil rights, America's poverty and space exploration. In 1977, he received the Presidential Medal of Freedom (the nation's highest peacetime award). He died in 1978 at the age of eighty-four.

Lynette Schmidt has illustrated a number of books for children including *The Day They Put a Tax on Rainbows*, *The Daddy Machine* and *The Duke Who Loved Jellybeans and Other Stories*, all published by Alyson Press.

Kitty Suen is Art Director of Theatre Communications Group and *American Theatre* magazine. She is a painter and graphic designer who resides in Brooklyn.

Adan Valdez was born in 1976, in the small Mexican town of San Sebastian. His art has been exhibited in many galleries in Texas, Mexico and England. Mr. Valdez recently designed the set for the annual CalArts Plaza de la Raza theatrical play, *Bags*. He is the founder of Utopia Entertainment, an indie film and concert production company.

Gabrielle Veit-Bermúdez is a photographer, illustrator and translator. She lives on a small orchard just west of downtown Los Angeles.

Andy Warhol was born in Pittsburgh in 1928. In 1945 he entered the Carnegie Institute of Technology where he majored in pictorial design. After graduation he moved to New York City and worked steadily as a commercial artist, and illustrated for magazines, such as *Vogue*, *Harper's Bazaar* and the *New Yorker*. He also did window displays and advertising for retail stores such as Bonwit Teller. A major figure of the 1960s Pop Art movement, his multiple images of Campbell Soup cans and Marilyn Monroe screenprints remain icons of twentieth-century art. During this period he also made many 16mm films, which have become underground classics. In the early 1970s he founded *Interview* magazine, and renewed his interest in painting, which continued through the 1980s. He died unexpectedly following routine surgery on February 22, 1987.

Kendra Wohlert is a music teacher who has just returned from two years in Peace Corps Africa. She is pursuing a graduate degree in Choral Conducting at Northern Arizona University.

USER'S GUIDE

I. For use in classroom or at home as a springboard for discussion or other interactive exercises.

A. Get acquainted with the plays, songs and poems in this anthology. The themes, by chapter are:

1. *My Family Tree Is a Garden!*: Love is what makes a family.

2. *Get to Know Me!*: Name-calling is never acceptable.

3. *Be Proud of Your Difference!*: Love and accept yourself and others. Celebrate what makes us each different, unique, special.

4. *We Can Change the World!*: Whether we stand alone or with others, if we're not part of the solution, we might be part of the problem.

B. Read aloud, with one or as many readers as seems appropriate.

1. Don't assign roles at first. Instead try reading round-robin style, that way children can play adults, boys play girls, and the class clown can play a teacher, even if just for a moment. It's an egalitarian way to let everyone get a crack at every role without worrying about why she or he has been selected to play the role. No one gets "stuck" with or deprived of any specific role—victim, bully or otherwise. This way things remain fluid, and everyone has an opportunity to walk in shoes she or he is unaccustomed to.

2. Read aloud at least one more time, giving children turns playing various roles, allowing them to read the roles and parts that interest them.

3. Explore with the children the many different ways that the plays and poems can be read aloud by using different combinations of speakers, playing with the word sounds, allowing some of the students to move while others read, etc.

C. Follow up with the exercises described in *Cootie Shots: Classroom Activities Against Bigotry for Educators Who Want to Make a Difference* (may be obtained for free through GLSEN in Los Angeles via their website: www.glsenla.org) and in Sharon Grady's *Drama and Diversity* (Portsmouth, NH: Heinemann, 2000).

D. After reading *Cootie Shots*, perform some of the plays for your school, community and/or faith group.

E. Create your own play, song or poem dealing with social justice issues in your school, community and/or faith group.

II. Performing the plays.

A. Dramaturgy.
When assembling a sampling of the plays to present as a "show," do not exclude any one diversity issue represented in the anthology—e.g., religion, disability, sexual orientation, etc. If it feels difficult to include one particular issue when performing for or within a certain community, that is probably a signal that it is *even more important* to include a play, poem or song about that issue to open dialogue with that community. While it is not always possible to give equal time to all diversity issues in one performance, it would not be in

keeping with the spirit of *Cootie Shots* to exclude any one issue a priori. From an educational standpoint, it is important for the youth to discover the points of connection between various diversity issues . . . and thereby our common ground as human beings. Presenting a sampling of pieces dealing with diverse issues to young audiences also helps them develop empathy with others. In one scene, a child might imagine herself as the target of the abuse, in the next the bully and, in the next, perhaps, the bystander who intervenes and helps.

B. Direction.

1. Casting.

    a. DIVERSITY!!!! (in terms of race, age, size, shape, ability, sexual orientation, religion, culture, etc.)

    b. Be careful not to reinforce stereotypes.

    c. When doing multiple plays, make sure the same actors do not always play bullies, good guys or targets, etc., or that people of one gender, race or size do not always play the bullies, good guys or targets.

    d. Children and/or adults can perform these plays.

2. Staging.

    a. Find ways to open up the text. For example, in *The Golden Rule*, where three of the four children wear religiously symbolic clothing and discuss their beliefs, it is helpful to consider what each of the children might be doing (e.g., reading or playing games by themselves, such as hopscotch, juggling, flying paper airplanes, etc.), and to stage this action at the start of the play. Fleshing out these details helps break down stereotypes and encourages the audience to feel familiar with the characters and to recognize them as individuals.

III. Advancing the work and Permissions.

A. **We understand that some scenes, in some circumstances, may need to be updated.** However, no internal edits are permitted on the pieces without express written permission from Fringe Benefits and from the author(s) of the specific piece(s) in question.

B. **Our intention is to make this book as user-friendly as possible.** Should you wish to present the plays for educational purposes or otherwise, simply contact Fringe Benefits (P.O. Box 691215, Los Angeles, CA 90069, email: normabowles@earthlink.net), and we'll help you as quickly as possible. In most cases, we require only proper credit for use.

C. **Fringe Benefits toured *Cootie Shots* from 1999–2001 using a small sampling of the plays, one for upper elementary, another for lower elementary, each presented to assemblies of no more than 250 children at a time.** A guided discussion with the audience was led by a trained facilitator between each scene. We highly recommend this format. At the end of each show the cast, crew and facilitator shared with the audience their experiences in elementary school (e.g., getting picked on for one thing or another, picking on others, intervening, etc.) and why they were doing the show. This helped kick off a fifteen-minute post-show discussion with the audience. We'll be happy to share our program and discussion outline with you.

FRINGE BENEFITS YOUTH THEATRE

F.B. (Fringe Benefits) Alliance Board of Directors:

Norma Bowles, President	Daisietta Kim
Kenneth Zahner, Treasurer	Barbara June Dodge Dart
M. Michele Manzella, Secretary	Laura Jane Salvato

History and Mission: Fringe Benefits is a Los Angeles-based educational theatre company, which has been helping youth enter into constructive dialogue on issues of tolerance and diversity since 1991. The company's previous productions have earned the commendations of educators, parents, community and religious leaders, as well as acknowledgment by the President's Committee on the Arts and Humanities. The work of Fringe Benefits is the subject of the book, *Friendly Fire* (A.S.K. Theater Projects, Los Angeles, 1997), and also of the feature documentary *Surviving Friendly Fire*, narrated by Sir Ian McKellan. Fringe Benefits' ever-expanding alliance includes professional theatre artists, educators, administrators, parents, therapists, activists and students of many different ages, ethnicities, religions, sexual orientations, classes, genders and abilities.

Programs: The members of Fringe Benefits work collaboratively and individually to create plays that celebrate diversity and promote tolerance. Our team of workshop leaders/performing artists also conducts interactive workshops wherein participants can develop constructive, imaginative ways to address discrimination. These performances and workshops have been enthusiastically received in schools, shelters, churches, theatres and community programs throughout California.

For more information, or to bring a FRINGE BENEFITS play or workshop to your school or community center *anywhere*, please email us at:
normabowles@earthlink.net
or write us at P.O. Box 691215, Los Angeles, CA 90069.

Cootie Shots' **Parent Guide**, researched and written by Ferdinand Lewis and translated into Spanish by Liane Schirmer of In Other Words Entertainment Translations, with the assistance of Ruben Amavizca of Grupo de Teatro Sinergia, can be obtained through Fringe Benefits.

Cootie Shots: **Classroom Activities Against Bigotry for Educators Who Want to Make a Difference**, edited by Steven Hicks, can be obtained through GLSEN/L.A. (Gay, Lesbian and Straight Education Network of Los Angeles), 1125 McCadden Place, Suite 105, Los Angeles, CA 90038, 323-460-4573, email *glsenla@glsenla.org*. Send check for $14 ($10 book, $4 shipping and handling), made out to GLSEN, or the entire guide may be downloaded for free from their website: *www.glsenla.org*.

Norma Bowles, Editor
Ms. Bowles is the Founder and Artistic Director of Fringe Benefits.
In addition to producing and directing many of Fringe Benefits'
shows, she also conducts many of the play development
workshops, edits the plays for production and facilitates school
tour performances. Ms. Bowles has conducted acting, commedia
dell'arte and new play development residencies at theatres and
universities throughout the U.S., including South Coast Repertory
(for nine years), the California Institute of the Arts and Walt
Disney Studios, and with the Melody Sisters of Spain. Ms. Bowles
has a B.A. in masked performance from Princeton University, an
M.F.A. in directing from the California Institute of the Arts and
Lecoq actor-training from Philippe Gaulier in Paris. She is a card-
carrying member of the Association for Theatre in Higher
Education; the Southern Poverty Law Center; the Gay, Lesbian,
Straight Education Network; and the National Council of
Education Activists.

Mark E. Rosenthal, Associate Editor
Writer, actor and director Mark E. Rosenthal has been a member
of Fringe Benefits since 1992. Mr. Rosenthal's relationship with
Fringe Benefits began when he was a resident of a youth shelter
sponsored by the Los Angeles Gay and Lesbian Community
Services Center. After a brief stay at Van Ness Recovery House,
Mark continued to work with Fringe Benefits as a writer and
actor. In addition, he was the Associate Project Director for
Cootie Shots. His work has been published in *Parabasis*, *Friendly
Fire* (both published by A.S.K. Theater Projects) and *Lesbian
News*. He was born in New York and now resides in Los Angeles.
He may be reached at diwractor@aol.com. Mark doesn't use his
middle initial to sound important; he has to because there are so
many other Mark Rosenthals in the world.

Bob Stern, Book Designer
Bob Stern works in most areas of the graphics arts field,
designing architectural signage, exhibitions, corporate and
institutional logos and identities, computer user interface,
and all kinds of publications. He studied architecture at
Princeton (where he met Norma), received an M.F.A. in graphic
design from Yale University, and studied typography in Italy
on a Fulbright scholarship. He lives in New York with his
partner and their one-year-old son. He can be reached at
Bob@the2bgroup.com.